Endangered
Animals

VOLUME 8

Pygmy-Possum, Mountain – **Siskin,** Red

GROLIER
EDUCATIONAL

Published 2002 by Grolier Educational, Danbury, CT 06816

This edition published exclusively for the school and library market

Produced by Andromeda Oxford Limited
11–13 The Vineyard, Abingdon,
Oxon OX14 3PX, U.K.
www.andromeda.co.uk

Principal Contributors: *Amy-Jane Beer, Andrew Campbell, Robert and Valerie Davies, John Dawes, Jonathan Elphick, Tim Halliday, Pat Morris. Further contributions by David Capper and John Woodward*

Project Director: *Graham Bateman*
Managing Editors: *Shaun Barrington, Jo Newson*
Editor: *Penelope Mathias*
Art Editor and Designer: *Steve McCurdy*
Cartographic Editor: *Tim Williams*
Editorial Assistant: *Marian Dreier*
Picture Manager: *Claire Turner*
Production: *Clive Sparling*
Indexers: *Indexing Specialists, Hove, East Sussex*

Reproduction by A. T. Color, Milan
Printing by H & Y Printing Ltd., Hong Kong

Set ISBN 0-7172-5584-0

Library of Congress Cataloging-in-Publication Data

Endangered animals.
     p. cm.
    Contents: v. 1. What is an endangered animal? -- v. 2. Addax -
blackbuck -- v. 3. Boa, Jamaican - danio, barred -- v. 4. Darter,
Watercress - frog, gastric brooding -- v. 5. Frog, green and golden bell -
kestrel, lesser -- v. 6. Kestrel, Mauritius - Mulgara -- v. 7. Murrelet,
Japanese - Pupfish, Devil's Hole -- v. 8. Pygmy-possum, mountain - Siskin, red -- v.
9. Skink, pygmy blue-tongued - tragopan, Temminck's -- v. 10. Tree-kangaroo,
Goodfellow's - zebra, mountain.
  ISBN 0-7172-5584-0 (set : alk. paper) -- ISBN 0-7172-5585-9 (v. 1 : alk. paper) –
ISBN 0-7172-5586-7 (v. 2 : alk. paper) -- ISBN 0-7172-5587-5 (v. 3 : alk. paper) –
ISBN 0-7172-5588-3 (v. 4 : alk. paper) -- ISBN 0-7172-5589-1 (v. 5 : alk. paper) –
ISBN 0-7172-5590-5 (v. 6 : alk. paper) -- ISBN 0-7172-5591-3 (v. 7 : alk. paper) –
ISBN 0-7172-5592-1 (v. 8 : alk. paper) -- ISBN 0-7172-5593-X (v. 9 : alk. paper) –
ISBN 0-7172-5594-8 (v. 10 : alk. paper)
  1. Endangered species--Juvenile literature. [1. Endangered species.] I. Grolier
Educational (Firm)

QL83 .E54 2001
333.95'42--dc21

00-069134

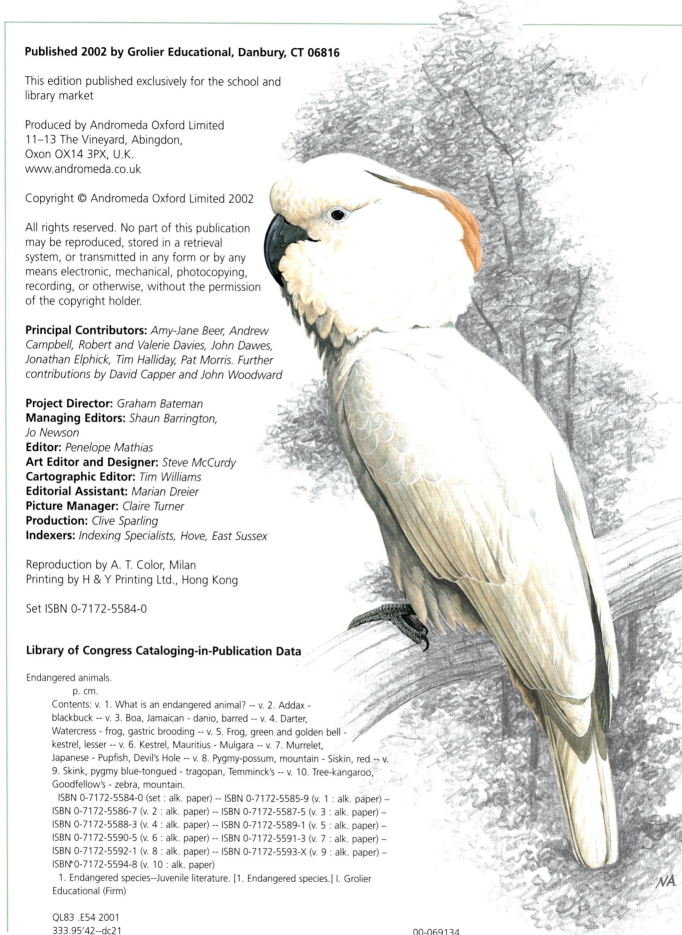

Contents

About This Set

Endangered Animals is a 10-volume set that highlights and explains the threats to animal species across the world. Habitat loss is one major threat; another is the introduction of species into areas where they do not normally live.

Examples of different animals facing a range of problems have been chosen to include all the major animal groups. Fish, reptiles, amphibians, and insects and invertebrates are included as well as mammals and birds. Some species may have very large populations, but they nevertheless face problems. Some are already extinct.

Volume 1—What Is an Endangered Animal?—explains how scientists classify animals, the reasons why they are endangered, and what conservationists are doing about it. Cross-references in the text (volume number followed by page number) show relevant pages in the set.

Volumes 2 to 10 contain individual species entries arranged in alphabetical order. Each entry is a double-page spread with a data panel summarizing key facts and a locator map showing its range.

Look for a particular species by its common name, listed in alphabetical order on the Contents page of each book. (Page references for both common and scientific names are in the full set index at the back of each book.) When you have found the species that interests you, you can find related entries by looking first in the data panel. If an animal listed under Related endangered species has an asterisk (*) next to its name, it has its own separate entry. You can also check the cross-references at the bottom of the left-hand page, which refer to entries in other volumes. (For example, "Finch, Gouldian **4:** 74" means that the two-page entry about the Gouldian finch starts on page 74 of Volume 4.) The cross-reference is usually made to an animal that is in the same genus or family as the species you are reading about; but a species may appear here because it is from the same part of the world or faces the same threats.

Each book ends with a glossary of terms, lists of useful publications and websites, and a full set index.

Pygmy-Possum, Mountain

Burramys parvus

Life in the snow-covered Victorian Alps is hard for the rare mountain pygmy-possum. The tourist industry is increasing the pressure, but conservation authorities are working to provide solutions.

When the mountain pygmy-possum was first discovered in 1864, zoologists were mistaken in two respects. Since the species was described from a few 15,000-year-old fossils found in a cave in New South Wales, it was thought to be already extinct. In addition, from the limited evidence available the new animal was classed as a kind of miniature kangaroo. In the 1950s a reexamination of the fossils concluded that the species was in fact a kind of possum. It appeared that the mountain pygmy-possum had once been widespread throughout southeastern Australia; but as the climate warmed up, the habitat of snow-covered boulder slopes and alpine heaths where the possums lived became scarce. Zoologists had no inkling that living specimens might still be scuttling around in the wild until 1966, when a real live mountain pygmy-possum turned up in a ski lodge at a resort on Mount Hotham in Victoria, southern Australia.

Hidden Creatures

As well as being extremely rare, the mountain pygmy-possum is, by nature, an inconspicuous mammal. It is small, nocturnal, and spends six months of the year hibernating in a boulder crevice under a thick layer of snow. It has a total range of no more than 4 square miles (10 sq. km). Its range is broken up into several parts, each area being separated by tracts of unsuitable habitat.

The needs of the mountain pygmy-possum are quite specific. It lives at high altitudes in order to take advantage of the arrival in spring of millions of bogong moths, which migrate to the Victorian Alps to breed. The moths are large and nutritious, and the possums time their own breeding to coincide with the glut of food. Later in the summer, as the moths disappear, the possums turn their attention to the berries and seeds of plants that only grow in their mountain heath habitat. Late summer and early fall see the possums feeding frantically. They need to double their body weight if they are to survive the winter. As an extra insurance policy, the possums are known to cache certain types of food, presumably so they can find it during their brief periods of winter activity, or if spring arrives late.

DATA PANEL

Mountain pygmy-possum

Burramys parvus

Family: Burramyidae

World population: Fewer than 3,000

Distribution: Southeastern New South Wales and northern Victoria, Australia

Habitat: Dense, subalpine boulder slopes at altitudes of 4,600–7,200 ft (1,400–2,200 m); among heath vegetation and snow-gum shrubs

Size: Length head/body: 4–5 in (10–13 cm); tail: 5–6 in (13–15 cm). Weight: 1–2 oz (30–60 g)

Form: Tiny, mouselike possum with distinct pouch and long, mostly hairless prehensile tail; eyes large and black; ears large and rounded; fur grayish brown above and whitish on underside

Diet: Seeds, fruit, worms, insects, and other invertebrates

Breeding: Up to 8 young born November–December after gestation of 13–16 days; maximum of 4 incubated in pouch; young leave pouch at 3 weeks, weaned at 8–9 weeks. Females may live up to 12 years, males 4 years

Related endangered species: Long-tailed pygmy possum (*Cercartetus macrurus*) LRnt

Status: IUCN EN; not listed by CITES

See also: Tourism 1: 42; Possum, Leadbeater's 7: 88; Rock-Wallaby, Prosperine 8: 36

A Fragile Existence

Despite all their preparation, many possums starve in winter; the death rate in males is four or five times as high as in females, simply because females occupy the best habitat. When they grow up, young males are driven out of their mother's home range and forced to live nomadic lives, eking out a living in marginal habitats. In spring they migrate back into female territories to mate.

Almost without exception, the areas in which the mountain pygmy-possum lives are prime sites for winter sporting activities, and efforts to conserve the species have required a good deal of negotiation and cooperation with the ski-tourism industry. Ski runs and roads break up areas of mountain pygmy-possum habitat and can present an almost impregnable barrier to migrating males. In order to give the possums a fighting chance, special tunnels have been constructed under existing roads and ski runs, providing migrating animals with alternative routes. Plans for further

Mountain pygmy-possums

are protected under state law in New South Wales and Victoria, and most of their range falls inside national parks. The species has been deleted from Appendix I of CITES, not because the possums are no longer endangered, but because there is no evidence of any attempt to trade them.

resorts are subject to intense scrutiny by conservation authorities. Several proposed resorts have had development permission denied on the grounds that they would be disruptive to the mountain habitat of the pygmy-possum.

Python, Woma

Aspidites ramsayi

According to Aboriginal folklore the woma python once roamed Australia in human form, creating the famous Ayers Rock and other mountains in Western Australia during a time known as "dreamtime" in the long-distant past.

The main woma territory is a large area in central Australia that takes in parts of Queensland, Northern Territory, South Australia, and New South Wales. Two populations of woma occur in Western Australia: one in the southwest, the other on the northwestern coast.

Little was known about the species until recently. Its habitat—mainly arid desert and scrubland—was sparsely populated, and the snake was considered rare until herpetologists (those who study reptiles and amphibians) began to observe it and found it to be more common than previously thought. In 1982 the first womas were bred in captivity. Since then it has become a popular species with hobbyists. It is good natured, not too large to accommodate, and reasonably easy to breed in captivity.

Coloration and size vary in woma pythons from different areas. The background color may be drab brown, yellowish, reddish brown, or olive, with darker brown crossbands of varying widths. The head can be light yellow or golden, and is usually unmarked, but in some individuals the juvenile head markings are retained. The snout is pointed, with the upper lip slightly overlapping the lower one. The protruding lip is possibly an adaptation for digging; the woma and its relative, the black-headed python, dig in loose soil using a scooping motion of the head. Unlike other pythons, woma and black-headed pythons do not have heat-detecting pits along the lips to sense warm-blooded prey. Much of their prey is ectothermic (cold-blooded) lizards and, occasionally, snakes.

Studying pythons in the wild in Australia has not been easy because of the vast areas involved, the difficult terrain, and the mainly nocturnal nature of the snakes.

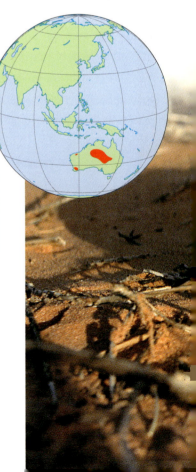

DATA PANEL

Woma python (Ramsay's python)

Aspidites ramsayi

Family: Boidae

World population: Unknown

Distribution: Central Australia: arid regions of Queensland, Northern Territories, South Australia, and Western Australia

Habitat: Arid and semiarid areas, including sand dunes, rocky regions, grasslands, woodlands, and scrub

Size: Length: adults usually 5 ft (1.5 m); occasionally up to 8 ft (2.5 m)

Form: Cylindrical body with short tail and vestiges of hind limbs; eyes with vertically elliptical pupils. Coloration brown, yellowish, reddish brown, or olive with darker brown bands; juveniles more intensively colored. Pointed snout

Diet: Mammals and reptiles (mainly lizards, occasionally snakes)

Breeding: One clutch of 6–19 eggs laid; female incubates eggs

Related endangered species: None

Status: IUCN EN; not listed by CITES

See also: Organizations 1: 10; Boa, Jamaican 3: 4; Boa, Madagascar 3: 6

Habitat Loss

Human activity is destroying the outer parts of the woma's range. There is no estimate for total numbers of woma pythons in the wild, but they are known to have declined in certain areas; the last specimen reported in New South Wales was in 1890.

In Queensland land clearance for agriculture and grazing is threatening much suitable habitat; the most severely threatened is the southwestern population of Western Australia. The last confirmed record of woma pythons in the area was in 1987, when a specimen was supplied to the Western Australia Museum.

A large part of woma habitat in Western Australia has been turned over to agriculture, and an area known as the wheatbelt has been increasing for many years. Urban expansion, road construction, and related activities such as crop spraying are all threats. Snakes are also victims of road kills because of their habit of basking on road surfaces. In addition, feral and domestic cats are known to kill snakes, although the extent of predation has not been assessed: An assessment would have to be made if captive-bred young were to be released.

In Captivity

Specimens owned by hobbyists tend to come from the central part of the woma's range. No southwestern womas are held in captivity, although illegally held specimens may exist.

The species as a whole is recognized as being in danger and is listed under government conservation legislation. Even so, snakes are not popular; about 80 percent of Australia's snakes are venomous, and many people are ready to kill snakes of any species, classing them all as deadly.

Herpetologists are trying to investigate the population numbers, particularly of the southwestern form (if it still exists). Conservation bodies and herpetological societies are also trying to increase public awareness and encourage reports of sightings. The Western Australia Amateur Herpetological Society has offered to set up a captive-breeding program at its own cost if any southwestern womas are found and provided that government permission is granted.

The woma, *like other pythons, is nonvenomous; all pythons kill their prey by constriction.*

Quagga

Equus quagga

A form of the common zebra, the quagga used to roam the South African grasslands, but during the 19th century was hunted to extinction for its meat and hide.

The common zebra occurs as various localized and distinct varieties, and the one in southern Africa was sufficiently distinct to have been considered a separate species. It was known as the quagga, a name that was based on the loud barking-coughing sound that all zebras make.

Like the common zebra, quaggas formed large herds to exploit the vast grasslands and to achieve safety in numbers when attacked by predators. It is said that they preferred to spend the night in areas of short grass where they could not be easily ambushed. In good feeding areas the herds would stay in the same region throughout the year. However, where the grazing was poor, the quagga migrated seasonally to find better feeding places.

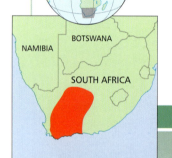

In the quagga *(above) the striping that is characteristic of all zebras was confined to the head, neck, and forequarters. Breeding experiments to produce an animal resembling the extinct quagga have included a cross between a mule and a zebra, to produce a "quagga" hybrid (right). However, this animal lacks the striped head and neck of the quagga and is gray, whereas the quagga was generally brown.*

The Road to Extinction

From about 1700 settlement in South Africa by Europeans increased substantially. By the late 19th century most of the land occupied by quaggas had

DATA PANEL

Quagga (Bonte quagga, Burchell's zebra)

Equus quagga

Family: Equidae

World population: 0 (Extinct)

Distribution: Formerly Cape Province and parts of Orange Free State, South Africa

Habitat: Dry temperate grasslands

Size: Length head/body: about 6 ft (2 m); tail: nearly 24 in (50–60 cm); height at shoulder: 4–5 ft (1.3–1.4 m). Weight: about 450 lb (200 kg); adult males can be up to about 650 lb (300 kg)

Form: Brown zebra in which the head, neck, and forequarters had brown and cream stripes, but the hind quarters were solid brown. As in other zebras, each individual had a slightly different pattern

Diet: Coarse grasses

Breeding: Single foal born probably after a gestation of about 1 year. Independent at 6–8 months and probably capable of breeding at 2–3 years. Life span may have been up to 40 years, as in common zebras today

Related endangered species: Mountain zebra (*Equus zebra*)* EN; Grevy's zebra (*E. grevyi*)* EN; African wild ass (*E. Africanus*) CR; Asiatic wild ass (*E. hemionus*) VU

Status: IUCN EX

See also: Speciation 1: 26; Genetics 1: 56; Zebra, Grevy's 10: 92; Zebra, Mountain 10: 94; Horse, Przewalski's Wild 5: 58

been brought into use for grazing livestock and for farming. The new settlers used to shoot quaggas for sport in far greater numbers than had ever been possible by the native people. The quaggas were killed by farmers as a convenient source of meat, and their skins also provided a source of strong leather, which was used for making robust bags. They were easy animals to hunt from horseback, since the open grassland offered nowhere to hide or escape. Hunting caused disruption of the quagga herds.

Although there may have been many surviving quaggas as late as the 1860s, they were scattered into small groups, which substantially reduced their breeding success. As the older animals died, there were too few offspring to replace them, and the last wild quagga was probably killed in about 1878. A few quaggas had been kept in zoos, the last individual dying in Amsterdam on August 12, 1883.

The only photographs of a living quagga are of the female that lived at the London Zoo from 1851 to 1872. Today there is only one quagga left on the entire continent of Africa—a preserved foal in the Cape Town Museum. About 22 stuffed and mounted specimens of adult quaggas are scattered among museums elsewhere.

Re-Creating the Quagga

It has been suggested that genetic material from some of the museum specimens might be used to clone a "re-created" quagga, but that will only be possible if the DNA has remained suitably preserved (tanning the skins, for example, which is part of the preservation process, harms DNA irrevocably). Experimental cross-breeding projects and the selective breeding of zebras with different coat patterns have also produced animals that look very similar to quaggas.

Quetzal, Resplendent

Pharomachrus mocinno

The resplendent quetzal is a symbol for conservation in Costa Rica and Panama. Although reserves have been established to protect it, the beautiful crested bird is at risk from the destruction and fragmentation of its forest habitat.

Males of the aptly named resplendent quetzal (pronounced "kets*aal*") are widely regarded as among the most beautiful of all the world's birds, along with the birds of paradise and the peacock. The species belongs to the colorful trogon family that is found across the tropics in Africa, Asia, and the Americas (with a few inhabiting temperate regions). There are five species of quetzal, all with helmetlike crests and elongated coverts (feathers that cover the wing and tail feathers).

As with other members of the trogon family, the male's plumage is much brighter than that of the females. The feathers making up the elongated tail-coverts are extremely flexible, so they flutter and undulate like some strange serpent behind the male's body as he performs his courtship displays in spring in order to attract a mate. The flexibility of the feathers also allows the male to bend them double and stick them out of the nest hole when he takes his turn at incubating eggs or feeding young.

Sacred Bird

It is not surprising that such a beautiful bird played a vital part in the mythology of early Central American peoples. It was revered as a sacred bird by the Aztecs of Mexico (who associated it with their wind god Quetzalcoatl) and also by the ancient Maya peoples of Guatemala. Its brilliant green feathers symbolized fertility, and only royalty and priests were allowed to display them in headdresses. The feathers were also used in trade as far north as New Mexico and as far south as the Andes. The bird was believed to be unable to survive in captivity, so it represented freedom. To obtain the plumes, male quetzals were trapped, then released unharmed to grow new feathers. It was forbidden to kill the bird, on punishment of death.

Cloud Forest Home

Aptly, this unusual bird lives in a special habitat: the evergreen cloud forest—a unique ecosystem found only at relatively high altitudes. Here the forest is immersed

DATA PANEL

Resplendent quetzal (resplendent trogon)

Pharomachrus mocinno

Family: Trogonidae

World population: Over 10,000 birds (estimated)

Distribution: Mountainous areas of southern Mexico, Guatemala, Honduras, El Salvador, Nicaragua, Costa Rica, and western Panama

Habitat: Montane cloud forests

Size: Length head/body: 14–15.75 in (36–40 cm); tail streamers: (male) up to 25.5 in (65 cm) longer

Form: Pigeon-sized, large-headed bird with large eyes and short, stout bill; short neck; compact body; short legs and feet. Male's plumage is mostly golden green to violet blue. A narrow, spiky, helmetlike crest extends forward to cover base of yellow bill. Female is duller, with bronzy head, bushy crest, green upperparts, and mainly brownish-gray underparts

Diet: Mainly fruit, especially avocado pears and fruit of other trees of the laurel family, as well as the blue fruit of *Symplocos*, figs, plums, and others (41 species of fruit recorded at 1 site); also some insects and occasionally small lizards or frogs

Breeding: In spring the female lays 2 greenish-blue eggs in an unlined hole, hacked out by both sexes in a rotting tree trunk 13–90 ft (4–27 m) above ground; the pair take turns incubating the eggs for about 18 days. The young fledge in about 17 days

Related endangered species: Nine other species of trogons are also Lower Risk, near threatened, including the eared quetzal (*Euptilotis neoxenus*)

Status: IUCN LRnt; CITES I

See also: CITES **1:** 12; Saving the Habitats **1:** 88; Bird of Paradise, Blue **2:** 84

in clouds for much of the time, so it is very wet. The moisture-laden air and water dripping from the leaves allow epiphytes (plants that grow on other plants) to flourish. The trees are festooned with luxuriant growths of mosses, lichens, mistletoes, bromeliads, and other epiphytes.

In the cloud forests the quetzals can find their staple food of wild avocados, which they swallow whole. They regurgitate the stones (large seeds) later, often some way from the original tree. The undigested seeds can still grow into new avocado trees. Resplendent quetzals are among the only fruit-eating birds able to eat such large fruit, and the birds and the avocados appear to have a high degree of mutual dependence.

Threats and Remedies

Today the quetzal is the national bird of Guatemala and has given its name to that nation's currency. It also appears on its flag and on postage stamps. In Costa Rica and Panama the bird is an important symbol for conservation, drawing many tourists and birdwatchers to the reserves set up to protect it.

However, the quetzal has suffered continuing declines due to deforestation. In Central America large areas of cloud forest have already been cleared, especially for growing coffee. Slash-and-burn agriculture by landless peasants has made the problem worse. Once a patch of cloud forest is cleared, the thin topsoil is quickly eroded.

It is not just the cloud forests that need protection. Studies in Costa Rica tracking birds with radio collars found that after breeding they moved to between 3,300 and 9,800 feet (1,000 and 3,000 m) on both Pacific and Atlantic slopes. These lower forests suffer even more from destruction than the cloud forests. For this reason it is vital to enlarge reserves and protect "corridors" between breeding and nonbreeding areas so that the birds can move between the habitats and further declines are prevented.

The resplendent quetzal *is the biggest and by far the most beautiful of all the quetzals. The male (above) is particularly stunning.*

Rabbit, Amami

Pentalagus furnessi

Originating from just two tiny Japanese islands, the Amami rabbit is a shy, forest-dwelling animal that is in need of consideration from forest managers and members of the public if it is to survive.

The Amami rabbit takes its name from the small Japanese island of Amami Oshima, which along with the even smaller neighboring island of Tokuno-shima, is the only place in the world where the species lives wild. The rabbits' island homes were once covered in dense, temperate forest, but since the 1950s large areas have been felled, the timber being used for making wood pulp.

The Amami rabbit feeds mostly on bamboo and pampas grass shoots that are abundant in patches of recently felled forest where sunlight is allowed to reach the ground. However, the rabbits are unwilling to venture far from the security of the dense forest cover, so they are unable to take advantage of large areas of clear-cut forest.

Mature forest is vital to the Amami rabbit's survival, not only because it offers cover, but because it also provides them with winter food. Shoots and leaves become scarce in winter; but as long as the rabbits have access to a good crop of acorns, they cope well. Nevertheless, once an area has been clear-cut, it will be at least a decade before any new trees produce enough winter food to support even a few rabbits. By that time many may have died from a lack of suitable foods.

Introduced Predators

The Amami rabbit's wariness is well justified, since it has many predators, the most significant of which are species introduced by humans. Domestic and feral (wild) cats and dogs and mongoose account for many premature rabbit deaths. The mongoose were deliberately released in the north of Amami Oshima for sport and appear to have wiped out the rabbits from a wide area. In the past the rabbits were hunted by people too, partly for their meat and fur, but also to supply the Eastern medicine trade with body parts. Such hunting is now banned, and the rabbit has been declared an animal of special significance by the Japanese government.

Another recent development pushed the struggling population on Amami Oshima one step

CHINA
RUSSIA
NORTH KOREA
SOUTH KOREA
JAPAN
Amami O-shima & Tokuno-shima

DATA PANEL

Amami rabbit (Amami hare, Ryukyu rabbit)

Pentalagus furnessi

Family: Leporidae

World population: About 2,500, spread across 2 islands

Distribution: Japan—only on 2 of the Ryukyu Islands (Amami Oshima and Tokuno-shima)

Habitat: Dense, temperate forests

Size: Length: 17–20 in (43–51 cm). Weight: 4.4–6.6 lb (2–3 kg)

Form: Medium-sized, thickset animal with warm-brown fur, almost black. Ears and legs short

Diet: Leaves and shoots, especially bamboo, pampas grass, and sweet potato; also acorns and some berries

Breeding: Two litters of 2 or 3 young born each year in underground burrow. Average life span probably about 1 year, but may live up to 10 years

Related endangered species: Volcano rabbit (*Romerolagus diazi*)* EN; hispid hare (*Caprolagus hispidis*)* EN; bushman hare (*Bunolagus monticularis*) EN; Sumatran hare (*Nesolagus netscheri*) CR

Status: IUCN EN; not listed by CITES

See also: Populations **1:** 20; Introductions **1:** 54; Hare, Hispid **5:** 50; Rabbit, Volcano **8:** 14

closer to extinction. New roads built across two peninsulas on the island cut off the rabbits on the peninsulas from the rest of the population; the animals were apparently unwilling to cross the expanse of open road. In ecological terms the enforced road barrier had the effect of isolating a section of the population on an even smaller "island" of habitat. As it turned out, the two fragments of forest were too small to support sustainable rabbit populations, and the peninsula rabbits are thought to have died out.

An Isolated Future

Most of the remaining wild Amami rabbits now live in one area in the center of Amami Oshima, with a few in the east and a couple of small populations on the island of Tokuno-shima. Species living on small islands are always vulnerable to extinction, but in the case of the Amami rabbit there are a number of straightforward measures that can be taken to increase the species' chances of survival.

It appears that logging in itself is not a serious threat, so long as the trees are taken down in small, scattered areas at a time—a process known as mosaic management. That will create small clearings where important rabbit foods like bamboo and pampas grass can flourish, but without destroying the trees that provide cover and the high-energy winter foods like nuts and acorns that the rabbits depend on. Steps should also be taken to control the populations of feral cats and mongoose, since that will remove another threat to the remaining rabbits.

Hispid hare
(Caprolagus hispidis) EN

Volcano rabbit
(Romerolagus diazi) EN

Sumatran hare
(Nesolagus netscheri) CR

Bushman hare
(Bunolagus monticularis) EN

Amami rabbit
(Pentalagus furnessi) EN

The Amami rabbit
is one of several species in the family Leporidae that are considered by the IUCN to be Critically Endangered or Endangered.

Rabbit, Volcano

Romerolagus diazi

The volcano rabbit is one of the world's rarest mammals, yet it lives within a short distance of one of the world's most densely populated human settlements: Mexico City.

The high ground overlooking the Valley of Mexico is studded with volcanoes, some more active than others. The lower southern slopes of the valley are dominated by natural forests of pine and alder, with a dense understory of scrub. At higher altitudes these forests give way to tussocky "zacaton" grassland made up of bunch grasses such as *Epicampes* and *Festuca* species. The volcano rabbit, or zacatuche, lives at the treeline, where the forests meet the zacaton.

The volcano rabbit has been rare for as long as records have been kept; whether the low numbers are due to natural causes or centuries of persecution is not certain. However, the rabbit's specialized habitat requirements suggest that it has never been widespread. The zacaton habitat is unique to this part of Mexico and is itself at risk.

Volcano rabbits are smaller than their more familiar cousins, but in other respects have much in common with them. For example, volcano rabbits are great diggers and, like their relatives, will also develop a network of overground runways that crisscross through the dense grass. The most important similarity from a conservation point of view, however, is the volcano rabbit's relationship with local farmers—the animal is just as unpopular in Mexico as North American cottontails and European rabbits are with farming communities in their ranges. Under normal circumstances the rabbits feed mainly on the new shoots of wild grasses, but the temptation of cultivated oats and corn is too much to resist; given the chance, they will readily take advantage of the bountiful food supply.

A Change of Image

Local people have long regarded the volcano rabbit as a pest, and their attempts to eradicate it have very nearly succeeded. The rabbits have never been hunted for meat, but farmers have seen them as pests and shot them indiscriminately. They were also used for target practice by quail hunters.

Grazing cattle compete with the rabbits for food, and

DATA PANEL

Volcano rabbit (zacatuche, teporingo)

Romerolagus diazi

Family: Leporidae

World population: About 1,000–1,200 (1964 estimate)

Distribution: Volcanic rim of the Valley of Mexico, near Mexico City

Habitat: Tussock grass on volcanic basalt at the edges of pine forests; found at altitudes of 9,200–14,000 ft (2,800–4,250 m)

Size: Length: 11–14 in (27–36 cm). Weight: 0.8–1.3 lb (390–600 g)

Form: Small and compact, with small ears and virtually no tail

Diet: Young zacaton grasses and leaves of other low-growing plants; bark from alder trees; some crops, including oats and corn

Breeding: Between 1 and 4 furry young born after gestation of 5–6 weeks at any time of year (with peak births in March–July); weaned at 3 weeks

Related endangered species: Amami rabbit *(Pentalagus furnessi)** EN; hispid hare *(Caprolagus hispidus)** EN; several other rabbit and hare species

Status: IUCN EN; CITES I

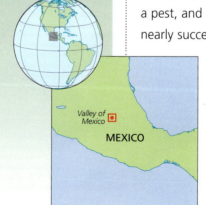

Valley of Mexico

MEXICO

See also: Biomes **1:** 18; Pasture **1:** 38; Pika, Steppe **7:** 74; Rabbit, Amami **8:** 12

their trampling feet alter the nature of the grasslands. The rabbits dig out their burrows and nests at the foot of big tussocks of grass. After heavy grazing these tussocks disappear, leaving the rabbits without shelter. The grasses are also harvested for thatch, becoming too closely cropped to offer cover from predators. Swathes of forest have been cleared, bringing settlements right up to the rabbits' habitat.

The volcano rabbits are now protected in several ways. The area where they live is designated as a national park. Hunting the rabbits is strictly illegal, although it undoubtedly still happens. The close proximity of Mexico City and the dramatic local scenery mean that the area is increasingly popular with

Volcano rabbits *look like smaller, slightly dumpier versions of their cousins, the North American cottontail and European rabbits, but their ears are noticeably smaller, and they have no powder-puff tail.*

tourists. The presence of tourists may help reduce incidences of illegal shooting. However, the increase in human traffic also brings a growing risk of forest fires. Before ecotourism projects can be set up, much remains to be done to encourage local people to respect a creature they currently view as vermin.

There are volcano rabbits in captivity. The British naturalist Gerald Durrell was one of the first to recognize the plight of the species; in the mid 1960s he established a small colony at Jersey Zoo in the Channel Islands, where the animals bred successfully for several years. Today volcano rabbit colonies are doing well in Mexico City Zoo and at other conservation centers in Mexico.

Racer, Antiguan

Alsophis antiguae

Together with the St. Lucia racer, the Antiguan racer has the dubious distinction of being one of the world's rarest snakes, with possibly just over 100 specimens surviving. Once common on mainland Antigua, it is now isolated on a tiny offshore island.

Antigua in the West Indies—one of the Leeward Islands—has a total area of 170 square miles (440 sq. km) and includes the island of Barbuda. The combined human population of Antigua and Barbuda is about 65,000, although Barbuda—a game reserve—has only about 1,500 inhabitants. Antigua is itself made up of over 50 small islands. Some are little more than rocky outcrops; others are forested or support pasture. Great Bird Island—with an area of only 96 square yards (80 sq. m)—is now the last remaining home of the Antiguan racer.

Antigua's story is typical of many Caribbean islands. The land was cleared for cultivation and domestic stock introduced. The introduced species played a significant part in the destruction of the native habitat and wildlife. Goats grazed many areas bare, pigs ate reptile eggs, and dogs and cats preyed on young animals. Rats soon followed the humans. The rats ate snake eggs and also lizards, the main food of racers. The rats eventually became such a pest on Antigua that in the 19th century mongoose were imported and released on some islands to eradicate them. The mongoose is also a notorious snake killer, so the Antiguan racer population was once again under pressure.

In spite of the damage caused by human settlement, many rare indigenous animals and plants survived, but only on the offshore islands. Today the local people are more aware that the native flora and fauna are assets, since the islands' main income is from tourism. However, tourism can itself be destructive to wildlife unless it is carefully controlled.

Field Studies

Little was known about the Antiguan racer when it first attracted the attention of conservationists. One of the tasks in the plan to save it was to estimate the population size and to study its ecology. Specimens were captured from the wild, marked, released, and recaptured in an attempt to estimate numbers. Some specimens were fitted with transmitters and tracked. It was discovered that the racers are terrestrial and are not expert climbers. During early studies there was confusion over the sexes. Males—which are smaller than females and have darker coloration—were at first thought to be a separate subspecies.

DATA PANEL

Antiguan racer

Alsophis antiguae

Family: Colubridae

World population: At least 90 in the wild

Distribution: Antigua

Habitat: Coralline limestone; hot, dry areas; low, deciduous woodland with grassland

Size: Length: males 32 in (80 cm); females 39 in (100 cm)

Form: Slender, smooth-scaled snake. Female is pale silvery gray with salmon-pink flush; back carries darker brown transverse bands or zigzag patterns. Male is darker—chocolate brown with paler bands

Diet: Lizards

Breeding: Between 3 and 6 eggs laid (in captivity)

Related endangered species: Black racer (*Alsophis ater*) CR; Leeward Island racer (*A. rijearsmai*) EN; red-bellied racer (*A. rufiventris*) EN

Status: IUCN CR; not listed by CITES

Virgin Islands (U.S./U.K.)

Puerto Rico (U.S.)

ST. KITTS & NEVIS

ANTIGUA & BARBUDA

Montserrat (U.K.)

Guadeloupe (France)

DOMINICA

Martinique (France)

ST. LUCIA

ST. VINCENT & THE GRENADINES

BARBADOS

GRENADA

A number of bodies cooperated in the study of the Antiguan racer, including Flora and Fauna International, the Environmental Awareness Group, the Forestry Unit of the Ministry of Agriculture, and the Island Resources Foundation. Fieldwork showed that numbers were low and that there were apparently no young specimens. Great Bird Island was found to be infested with rats that were evidently eating the snakes' eggs or killing the hatchlings. The situation required drastic measures.

Racers in Reserve

Five adult racers were flown to Jersey Wildlife Preservation Trust in Britain. The plan was to establish a "reservoir" population for reintroduction into the wild once the habitat had been restored. Meanwhile, a rat-eradication program using poisoned bait was getting underway. A further survey found improved vegetation, a plentiful supply of birds and lizards, and an increase in the number of racers—including

Antiguan racers *are slender snakes with smooth scales. Like all racers, they are relatively fast-moving and can achieve speeds of about 3.5 miles per hour (5.6 km/h).*

juveniles. In 1996 staff at Jersey Wildlife Preservation Trust used data gathered in field studies to replicate conditions in the wild and successfully hatched five baby racers, although one later died.

Captive breeding has been relatively successful, but there are no plans to release the young at present. Conservation revolves around keeping the island free of predators and eradicating rats on nearby islands that might provide alternative habitats. In November 1999 a "seed population" was moved from Great Bird Island to another island; radio tracking showed them to be thriving, and further translocations are planned. The snakes on Great Bird Island are doing well, and their immediate prospects for the future look good. However, any species with such a restricted habitat is always going to be under pressure.

17

Rail, Guam

Gallirallus owstoni

The flightless Guam rail has been completely wiped out in the wild by a species of snake that was accidentally introduced to its only home, the small Pacific island of Guam.

The Guam rail belongs to the same family as the more familiar gallinules and coots that are to be seen on freshwaters across much of the world. Living on a remote island, the Guam rail evolved in an environment where it did not need to fly because there were no predators. While life on the island remained unchanged, the rails were safe; but as soon as settlers arrived—accompanied by predatory animals—the birds' flightlessness and lack of fear made them easy prey. As a result, the rail family has probably lost more species in recent times than any other family of birds; at least 22 endemic species of flightless rail have become extinct since 1600.

The story of the Guam rail is unusual. Other island rails were wiped out mainly by introduced mammals such as rats and cats (and sometimes by habitat destruction). However, the Guam rail was made extinct in the wild by a species of snake.

Once Abundant

The small coral island of Guam is the largest and most southerly of the Mariana Islands. The islands lie to the north of Australia and New Guinea, in the western Pacific Ocean, and are dependent territories of the United States.

The Guam rail was once widely distributed across the island and found in most habitats there. It lived a secretive life, spending most of its time hidden deep in cover, emerging only at dawn and dusk to search for insects and to bathe in rain puddles at the edges of fields and roads.

Numbers were known to fluctuate with cycles of rainfall. However, the Guam rail was abundant, despite being hunted by the islanders using dogs and snares. Predation by introduced mammals such as cats and pigs was also a hazard. From the mid-1940s the population increased, and by the early 1960s there were thought to be about 80,000 birds on the island.

DATA PANEL

Guam rail (Owston's rail)

Gallirallus owstoni

Family: Rallidae

World population: 180 birds

Distribution: Native to Guam in the Mariana Islands in the western Pacific Ocean; now reintroduced to Guam and Rota Island

Habitat: Formerly most habitats on Guam, including forest, scrub, savanna, grassland, thickets of ferns, and agricultural land

Size: Length: about 11 in (28 cm). Weight: 6–10.6 oz (170–303 g); female smaller

Form: Pigeon-sized, stout-bodied, flightless bird; short tail with fragmented feathers. Plumage chocolate-brown above; broad pale stripe above eye; wings have black-and-white bars; chin and throat whitish; foreneck to upper breast pale gray; olive-buff breast band in freshly molted plumage; rest of underparts black with narrow white bars; eyes with red irises; daggerlike bill; legs and feet pale brown

Diet: Snails (especially introduced giant African snail), slugs, insects, and small geckos; some plant matter (seeds and flowers from low shrubs and grasses, melons, tomatoes, and palm leaves); also carrion

Breeding: All year round; peaks during rainy season of July–November. Nest built by both parents: shallow cup of interwoven, still-rooted living grasses and plucked loose grass; 1–4 (usually 3 or 4) white to pink eggs, spotted with red or blue, incubated by both sexes for 19 days; black downy chicks leave nest 24 hours after hatching, fed and cared for by both parents; mature at 4 months

Related endangered species: Thirty-three rail species, including New Caledonian rail (*Gallirallus lafresnayanus*) CR; Lord Howe rail (*G. sylvestris*) EN; takahe (*Porphyrio mantelli*)* EN; and corncrake (*Crex crex*)* VU

Status: IUCN EW; not listed by CITES

See also: Introductions 1: 54; Captive Breeding 1: 87; Coot, Horned 3: 62; Corncrake 3: 66; Takahe 9: 48

The Guam rail *emerges only at dawn and dusk to search for food. Predation of its eggs and young by tree snakes has brought about its extinction in the wild.*

Rapid Decline

After 1968 the Guam rail showed a decline in numbers, along with other birds that were indigenous to the island, and native species of bats and lizards. By 1981 there were only an estimated 2,000 rails left. At first zoologists were puzzled about the reasons for the catastrophe and investigated a range of possible causes, including habitat degradation, disease, and parasites. Eventually, the culprit was identified: the brown tree snake, a 10-foot- (3 m-) long nocturnal, tree-climbing, venomous species native to northeastern Australia, New Guinea, and nearby islands. Accidentally introduced to Guam in cargo shipments after World War II, by 1982 the formidable predator had become abundant across almost the entire island.

Although the snake seemed to find the adult rails too big to tackle, it decimated the bird's eggs and young. In 1976 the Guam rail was listed as a protected species; but of course this did not deter the snakes. By 1983 there were estimated to be fewer than 100 birds, and by 1987 the Guam rail was declared Extinct in the Wild.

Hope for a Safe Future

Fortunately, the Guam rail breeds well in captivity, and a captive-breeding program has been in place since 1982. Currently, there are about 180 birds in Guam and in 14 zoos in the United States. Although there does not seem to be any immediate danger of the species disappearing completely, attempts at establishing a viable breeding population in the wild depend entirely on protecting the birds from the tree snakes and, where possible, eliminating the snakes. Tree snake numbers are being reduced in places by trapping, but it is a slow process. There is an additional bonus for the islanders in removing the snakes, since they have a potent venom. As well as injuring people, they have killed chickens and caused power failures by climbing onto electricity cables and into transformers.

Since 1987 conservationists have been trying to establish a self-sustaining population of the rails on the island of Rota, to the north of Guam, which is free of snakes. Although early attempts failed, the birds bred there for the first time in 1999. In late 1998 captive-bred rails were released into an area in northern Guam kept free of snakes by trapping and a barrier; the released birds are now also breeding.

Rainbowfish, Lake Wanam

Glossolepis wanamensis

Near the eastern coast of Papua New Guinea, some 15 miles (24 km) west of Lae, there is a small lake that once contained millions of rainbowfish. During the late 1990s the Lake Wanam rainbowfish was thought to be extinct, but surveys have confirmed its reappearance in the lake. Today, despite captive-breeding programs, the rainbowfish is still Critically Endangered.

The rainbowfish of the family Melanotaeniidae are found in Australia and New Guinea. Named because of the wonderful array of colors exhibited by fully mature males of many of the species, rainbowfish are popular with aquarists the world over.

Alarming Decline

The Lake Wanam rainbowfish was first described scientifically in 1979. Within a few years it had become popular with specialized aquarists in several countries, owing both to its "newness" and its different coloration when compared to the well-known salmon-red rainbowfish from Lake Sentani in Irian Jaya (New Guinea).

Breeding *Glossolepis* rainbowfish in captivity is relatively easy. As a result, the majority of such fish in hobby aquariums come from large-scale commercial breeding enterprises and the efforts of dedicated enthusiasts. It would appear therefore that the wild population of Lake Wanam rainbowfish was not placed under a significant threat from overcollection.

In 1995 the news of the staggering decline in the Lake Wanam rainbowfish population was received with great alarm. For a number of years it had been known that the population levels of three exotic (nonnative) species had been rising significantly in the lake. However, it was not until 1995 that the effect which they were cumulatively exerting on the rainbowfish became fully apparent: A search yielded only two old male specimens. The situation was brought to public notice in 1998 by German collector and author Heiko Bleher, who had carried out a number of surveys of the lake between 1992 and 1995. During this period Bleher had observed a dramatic shift in abundance between the exotic and native rainbowfish.

The first of the exotics—the mosquito fish—had been introduced into Papua New Guinea in March 1930 as a biological means of controlling the malaria mosquito. As with other introductions elsewhere, this aggressive, invasive, highly adaptable, and prolific

DATA PANEL

Lake Wanam rainbowfish

Glossolepis wanamensis

Family: Melanotaeniidae

World population: Unknown; once believed extinct, but now bred in captivity; also now breeding in the lake

Distribution: Lake Wanam, Papua New Guinea

Habitat: Clear-water lake with vegetation around the edge

Size: Length: male up to 5.1 in (13 cm); female a little smaller

Form: A highly "compressed" fish; male develops a deep body; large eyes set in a pointed head. Fully mature male develops iridescent (glistening with a rainbow sheen) green-golden scales along the body. Unpaired fins carry some of the same basic coloration. Female is drab in color and does not have such a deep body

Diet: Wide range of food items taken, including small aquatic invertebrates and vegetation

Breeding: Eggs scattered among vegetation over a number of days rather than in a single spawning event. Hatching takes place 6–7 days later

Related endangered species: Ramu rainbowfish (*Glossolepis ramuensis*) DD; red rainbowfish (*G. incisus*) VU; Tami River rainbowfish (*G. pseudoincisus*) DD

Status: IUCN CR; not listed by CITES

New Guinea

INDONESIA

PAPUA NEW GUINEA

Lake Wanam

AUSTRALIA

See also: Communities and Ecosystems 1: 22; Introductions 1: 54; Cichlids, Lake Victoria Haplochromine 3: 48; Goby, Dwarf Pygmy 5: 34

species, not only eliminated mosquito larvae, but also decimated stocks of native fish species by competing with them for food and space and by preying on their eggs and offspring.

The second exotic, *Tilapia*, was introduced in 1954. It was soon deemed not just good to eat but to be an even more efficient mosquito controller than the mosquito fish. *Tilapia* are not renowned predators but they are versatile and flexible; they can spread with astonishing speed and in the process alter habitats to such an extent that they can become unsuitable for endemic species. The third species, carp, had an even greater capacity for altering habitats. Arriving in 1959, its presence also had a bad carryover effect. As a result, and for a time, it was believed that the Lake Wanam rainbowfish had become extinct in the wild.

Population Pendulum Swing

In 1998, following publication of the Bleher report, the Australian New Guinea Fishes Association (ANGFA), Melbourne Zoo, and the Rainforest Habitat (based in Lae, Papua New Guinea) agreed to try to prevent the total loss of the Lake Wanam rainbowfish. One of the first tasks undertaken by the Lake Wanam Management Project was a new survey of the lake.

Discussions with local people confirmed that there had been a virtual disappearance of the species at the

The Lake Wanam rainbowfish *seems surprisingly resilient. Perhaps this freshwater species' tolerance of extreme conditions may have saved it from extinction.*

time of earlier surveys. However, quite unexpectedly the new survey also revealed substantial numbers of the lake rainbowfish and showed that there had been a sharp decline in the *Tilapia* population.

Large-scale fishing for *Tilapia* by the fast-rising human population around the lake, while possibly affecting stocks, could not in itself explain the high losses. It is likely that a severe drought that hit the area in 1997 lowered lake water levels and caused water temperatures to rise. This apparently resulted in the deaths of thousands, if not millions, of fish, including *Tilapia*. However, the rainbowfish's inherent high-temperature tolerance would have helped it survive this critical period.

As a safeguard against future declines, some rainbowfish specimens were removed during the 1998 survey and are known to be reproducing satisfactorily in captivity. With other captive-bred populations as well as ongoing reproductive success within the lake itself, it is hoped that the species will now have a more secure future.

Rasbora, Vateria Flower

Rasbora vaterifloris

The dark, shady forest streams of southwestern Sri Lanka contain a wealth of beautiful and interesting fish species. One of them is a small rasbora, a freshwater tropical fish that is famous the world over among aquarists. While the fish is known to be a prolific breeder in the wild, it presents considerable challenges for captive breeding.

Also known as the fire, pearly, or golden rasbora, the vateria flower rasbora is a species named after a flower—but apparently after the wrong flower! The Sinhalese name for the vateria flower rasbora translates as the "hal flower rasbora." *Hal* is a tree, known scientifically as *Vateria acuminata* (hence vateria and the *vaterifloris* of the rasbora's scientific name). *Vateria acuminata* bears white or cream-colored blooms. According to a leading authority on Sri Lankan fish, it is quite conceivable that the scientist who officially described the vateria flower rasbora in 1930 confused the Sinhalese word *hal* with the similar sounding *sal*. *Sal* is the Sinhalese name for the cannonball tree—*Courouptia guianensis*, a South American species that was introduced into Sri Lanka in 1881; it bears blooms that are a similar shade to the dorsal (back) fin of the vateria flower rasbora.

A Variable Species

Despite its relatively restricted distribution (in global terms), at least four different color forms of the vateria flower rasbora are known to occur naturally in southwestern Sri Lanka. From north to south these varieties (which are regarded as subspecies by some authorities) are: *Rasbora vaterifloris vaterifloris* from the Kalu River Basin; *Rasbora vaterifloris ruber* from the Bentota River Basin; *Rasbora vaterifloris pallida* from the Gin River Basin; and *Rasbora vaterifloris rubriculis* from the Nilwala River Basin.

Color by itself is not usually regarded as a sufficiently valid criterion for a fish or any other animal

INDIA

SRI LANKA

DATA PANEL

Vateria flower rasbora (fire rasbora, pearly rasbora, golden rasbora)

Rasbora vaterifloris

Family: Cyprinidae

World population: Unknown; relatively abundant where it is found, but distribution is restricted

Distribution: Kalu, Bentota, Gin, and Nilwala river basins, southwestern Sri Lanka

Habitat: Small, shady, shallow forest streams, often with a silty base and a layer of leaf debris on the bottom

Size: Length: 1.6 in (4 cm), but often smaller

Form: Body slender, although female is rounder than male. Whole body has pearly sheen. Base color greenish brown on back, fading to orange down side of body and silvery orange on belly. Fins are orange-red. Eyes are large and have golden-red iris and a vertical black stripe running through pupil

Diet: Mainly small insects, aquatic invertebrates, and debris

Breeding: Prolific breeder in the wild. An energetic courtship results in numerous batches of about 20 eggs being scattered among fine-leaved or marginal vegetation. The spawning sequence may last for 30 minutes. Hatching takes about 1.5 days

Related endangered species: None, but nearly 300 other cyprinid species are being closely monitored by the IUCN

Status: IUCN LRcd; not listed by CITES

See also: Captive Breeding **1:** 87; Barb, Bandula **2:** 52; Danio, Barred **3:** 94

The vateria flower rasbora, *a member of the carp family, has large eyes and a protruding lower jaw.*

to be classified as a separate species or even subspecies. Other factors—such as skeletal differences—are also necessary. However, in the four above-mentioned instances there are no preserved and recorded specimens for use as "type" material. Such reference material—if it did exist—could help validate (or otherwise) the subspecific status of the fish. In the absence of type material it is generally agreed that the vateria flower rasbora is a single, variable species, with no subspecies.

Threefold Threat

There are three main threats to the vateria flower rasbora in the wild: deforestation, pollution, and collection. Deforestation removes the forest cover and thus the shade that the vateria flower rasbora seems to need for long-term survival (probably because such vegetation is the main source of insects and other invertebrates on which the fish feeds). Deforestation also results in increased levels of light and higher water temperatures, which the rasbora dislikes. By

eliminating leaf fall, it also deprives the rasbora of two other essential ingredients: soft, acidic water and leaf debris at the bottom of the streams.

A further detrimental effect of deforestation is that it is almost invariably accompanied by increased runoff (rainfall that is not absorbed by the soil) into the surrounding watercourses. The main dangers of such runoff are higher levels of pesticides and fertilizers in the water and increased siltation (the vateria flower rasbora likes clear water). Siltation and runoff in turn lead to deterioration in water quality.

Collection of the fish for aquaria was in the past also a potentially serious factor, particularly because the species, while breeding profusely in the wild, could not be bred in captivity on a commercial basis. However, as our knowledge of the species improves, so do the chances of breeding success. Several programs are currently underway in Sri Lanka with the aim of breeding the vateria flower rasbora on a regular basis and in commercial quantities.

The instigation of breeding programs, together with controls over the levels of capture and export of the species and the fact that the species is relatively abundant in its native waters, means that the future of the vateria flower rasbora looks a little more promising than it once did.

Rat, Black

Rattus rattus

Black rats are potentially harmful pests that have become rare in some areas. Their situation raises a conservation dilemma: Should we say "good riddance" to such pests and let them die out, or should we give them protection?

The black rat is not a threatened species in all parts of its range. In some parts of the world it is abundant and regarded as a serious pest. In the Caribbean and Pacific, for example, it attacks coconuts, sugarcane, cocoa, and other valuable crops. Elsewhere, especially on islands, it is a danger to rare species of reptile and nesting birds. The black rat's preference for living in houses and food supplies brings it into close contact with people, eating their food and contaminating it with droppings and urine. Rats have harbored and transmitted numerous diseases to humans, and a flea that occurs on the black rat is responsible for passing on the bubonic plague, an infectious disease that killed millions of people during the Middle Ages.

Originally from Southeast Asia, the black rat had spread to Europe by the Middle Ages, to South America by about 1550, and to the United States soon afterward. It is now widespread there in the southern and western states, particularly around ports along coasts and rivers.

Decline of the Stowaway

The black rat's ability to climb, jump, and burrow has made it a constant if unpopular companion of humans. The animals used to scramble aboard ships by way of gangplanks and mooring ropes. Consequently, they spread widely across the world and earned the alternative common name "ship rats." However, despite its abundance at the global level, the black rat has now become extinct over large parts of its former range. For example, it was the commonest rat in Britain for hundreds of years, but has now become one of that country's rarest mammals; there are only a few hundred left, mostly confined to two islands, Lundy (off southwestern England) and the Shiants off Scotland. The black rat has died out in many parts of Eastern Europe, although it is still common in the ports along the Danube River. It became extinct in Scandinavia, except for one locality in Denmark. It almost died out in the Netherlands, but since the 1970s it has been recovering and has adopted a new habitat: pig farms.

The reasons for the decline of the black rat include the fact that the species is best adapted to warm, dry conditions, and

DATA PANEL

Black rat (roof rat, climbing rat, gray rat, ship rat, Alexandrine rat)

Rattus rattus

Family: Muridae

World population: Millions

Distribution: Widespread across the world, but mostly in coastal regions associated with seaports

Habitat: Towns, buildings, forests, and farmland

Size: Length head/body: 6–9.5 in (15–24 cm); tail: 4.5–10 in (11.5–26 cm). Weight: 5–10 oz (145–280 g)

Form: Typical rat, with tail 30% longer than head and body. Often black, but sometimes gray or grayish brown with lemon-yellow belly

Diet: Almost anything edible

Breeding: Up to 16 young per litter (average 7); 3–5 litters per year. Life span up to about 2 years

Related endangered species: Numerous mice, mole-rats, and other members of the family Muridae

Status: Not listed by IUCN; not listed by CITES

See also: Generalist Species **1:** 29; Introductions **1:** 54; Mouse, St. Kilda **6:** 92

many of the countries it has invaded are unsuitable. More significantly, the spread of the Norway rat (also known as the brown, barn, sewer, or wharf rat) has exposed it to competition from a larger and even more successful species. Generally, black rats have retreated in the face of the new invader.

Human Enemies

Most significant of all, however, is the war that humans have waged against rats for centuries. When only traps and cats were being used, the rats could breed sufficiently fast to replace the losses. However, from the 1940s onward highly toxic poisons have been deployed against the animals, capable of removing all of them, especially from indoor environments. As a result, numbers of black rats have sharply declined, and in some areas the species has been completely exterminated.

Most people would probably like to get rid of the black rat; there might be a public outcry if a "Save the Black Rat" campaign was launched. However, the black rat's situation raises the question: Should we treat an animal we do not like differently from any other declining species? Does the black rat have the same right to exist as the panda, for example? Should it face extinction simply because it threatens the interests of humans?

The black rat *is an excellent climber and jumper. Modern poisons have drastically reduced the numbers and distribution of black rats, although since the 1970s they may have begun to develop genetic resistance to the commonest type of rat poisons.*

Rhinoceros, Black

Diceros bicornis

Formerly abundant and widespread in Africa, the black rhinoceros has been drastically reduced in numbers since the 1970s. The main culprit is the expanding international trade in rhino horn.

Although the black rhinoceros is able, if necessary, to go for five days without water, it is generally found in relatively moist areas of lush vegetation. Throughout Africa these regions are under pressure for development into farm and grazing land, effectively excluding the rhinos, which are too large and unpredictable to be tolerated close to human settlements. Yet the main threat to the animals comes not so much from habitat loss as from hunting, principally for their horns for use in oriental medicine.

For centuries rhino horn, composed of densely compressed hair, has been powdered and swallowed as a remedy for fevers and other disorders. It is made of keratin (a fibrous substance that occurs in skin, hair, nails, and hooves) and cannot be absorbed into the body, so any supposed medicinal benefits will only be imaginary. Yet the horns continue to fetch high prices, often earning more than their weight in gold.

In recent years a new factor has further complicated the situation. In Yemen in southwestern Asia there has long been a tradition of using rhino horn to make carved dagger handles. As oil money brought new prosperity to the region, the demand for these prestigious status symbols increased; in 1999 more than 100 craftsmen were employed in making and repairing such artifacts. Old and new horns were used; at the time, new horns were said to be fetching $615 per pound ($1,350 per kg), 20 percent more than they had only two years earlier.

Before hunting reduced their numbers, black rhinos could be found in the bush and savanna regions of most of Africa south of the Sahara. By the 1960s they were already becoming rare, but were still widely distributed, with substantial numbers in Kenya,

Tanzania, and Zimbabwe. Although the animals enjoyed legal protection, the lucrative trade in horns could not be controlled, and the rhino died out in one area after another as hunting took its lethal toll.

Slow Breeders

The black rhino has one of the slowest reproductive rates of any large mammal, making it ill-equipped to cope with population loss. Young animals first breed at five or even 10 years, but in practice many are killed long before they reach that age. Calves are not born annually, but at intervals of up to five years. In the past this was not a disadvantage; the slow breeding rate was probably a natural adaptation to avoid producing more young than the available resources could support. Excessive hunting has, however, overwhelmed the animal's capacity to maintain its numbers, which have fallen by more than 90 percent since 1970. The total figure now seems to have stabilized, but several countries where the species was

See also: CITES **1:** 12; Hunting **1:** 42; Luxury Products **1:** 46; rhinoceros species **8:** 28–35

Black rhinos *are usually tolerant of each other, but can be aggressive toward humans. Their temperamental behavior makes them difficult to manage; incidents involving rogue animals do not help the species' cause.*

once common now have fewer than 50 black rhinos, most of them confined to national parks and reserves.

Thanks to the high cash value of the horns, the killing continues; a poacher can earn more from one dead rhino than from a year's farmwork. One possible solution might be to remove the horns, which contain no nerve endings and can be painlessly cut away without disrupting the rhino's life. However, the horns grow back, so the process would have to be repeated. Even so, such a program would remove the incentive for poaching and might prove more practicable in the long run than captive breeding, which is the only other way of ensuring the rhino's long-term survival.

DATA PANEL

Black rhinoceros

Diceros bicornis

Family: Rhinocerotidae

World population: About 2,550 (1994 estimate)

Distribution: Africa south of the Sahara, in widely scattered localities

Habitat: Bush and savanna; rarely found more than a day's walk from water

Size: Length head/body: 9.5–12.3 ft (2.9–3.7 m); tail: 24–28 in (60–70 cm); height at shoulder: 4.5–5.9 ft (1.4–1.8 m). Weight: 1,500–3,000 lb (700–1,400 kg)

Form: Large, thick-skinned animal; grayish in color but often coated with dust or mud. Two horns on the snout and a pointed, mobile upper lip, used like a miniature trunk to gather food

Diet: Leaves, twigs, and branches browsed from more than 200 species of low-growing shrub

Breeding: Single calf born after 15-month gestation; suckled for up to 1 year. Life span may exceed 40 years

Related endangered species: White rhinoceros (*Ceratotherium simum*)* LRcd; great Indian rhinoceros (*Rhinoceros unicornis*)* EN; Javan rhinoceros (*R. sondaicus*)* CR; Sumatran rhinoceros (*Dicerorhinus sumatrensis*)* CR

Status: IUCN CR; CITES I

Rhinoceros, Great Indian

Rhinoceros unicornis

Despite its armor-plated appearance, the single-horned great Indian rhinoceros is vulnerable and has suffered badly from hunting as well as from habitat loss; it is now restricted to a handful of game reserves.

The Indian rhinoceros likes wet places where it can wallow in mud during hot weather, and where sufficient food is available to support its huge bulk. It feeds and shelters in the long scrub and grass habitats found on the wide plains that fringe the rivers of northern India. However, such fertile areas also make prime farmland, and over the last 300 years the rhino's habitat has been increasingly cultivated to grow crops. The expansion of human activity quickly proved incompatible with the continued presence of the animals, which not only ate vast amounts but could also be very aggressive, especially females with young calves to protect. As a result, the rhinos were forced out of their ancestral breeding grounds. For a while, there was even a government bounty paid for each rhino killed, as a measure to reduce the damage they caused in new tea plantations.

There were other motives for killing the rhinos. In India, as elsewhere, animals were slaughtered and their horns sold to the oriental medicine trade. In addition, many were killed by both Indian and European hunters for trophies; one maharajah (Hindu prince) is said to have shot over 200 animals in 30 years.

By the beginning of the 20th century the rhinos had gone from Pakistan and northwestern India and were becoming scarce in other parts of their range. About a dozen were left in what is now the Kaziranga National Park, and a few isolated individuals survived in other parts of India. There were only about 50 left in Nepal, where the species faced imminent extinction. Since that time, however, strict protection and the careful management of sanctuaries have slowly allowed the rhinos to recover. Yet there is still too little habitat for their numbers to build up to any great

DATA PANEL

Great Indian rhinoceros

Rhinoceros unicornis

Family: Rhinocerotidae

World population: About 2,300

Distribution: Bhutan, Nepal, and parts of northern India (Assam). Now extinct in Bangladesh

Habitat: Marshy areas of long grass; various types of forest

Size: Length head/body: 12–12.5 ft (3.6–3.8 m); tail: 28–32 in (70–80 cm); height at shoulder: 5.6–6 ft (1.7–1.8 m). Weight: 3,300–4,400 lb (1,500–2,000 kg); males can weigh up to 4,840 lb (2,200 kg)

Form: A huge animal whose knobby-looking skin hangs in large, stiff sections like sheets of armor plate. There is only 1 horn, up to 20 in (52 cm) long

Diet: Grasses, leaves, and aquatic plants; sometimes raids crops

Breeding: A single calf is born after a gestation of nearly 16 months. Weaning takes more than 1 year, and young are born only once every 3 years. Females can breed at 4 years, but males take 9 years to reach maturity. Life span about 40 years

Related endangered species: Black rhinoceros (*Diceros bicornis*)* CR; white rhinoceros (*Ceratotherium simum*)* LRcd; Javan rhinoceros (*Rhinoceros sondaicus*)* CR; Sumatran rhinoceros (*Dicerorhinus sumatrensis*)* CR

Status: IUCN EN; CITES I

See also: CITES **1**: 12; Hunting **1**: 42; rhinoceros species **8**: 26–35

extent, and illegal hunting is also difficult to stamp out. Rhino horns still fetch large sums of money, a huge temptation for poor villagers who cannot easily make a living from farming. In addition, the skin and blood of the rhinos are all said to have medicinal properties, further increasing the poachers' rewards.

Action against Poaching

In the early 1990s large amounts of money, both from local sources and international conservation organizations, enabled India and Nepal to implement action against poachers. Fines were introduced for traders in rhino body parts, and there were heavy jail sentences for hunters; several poachers were even shot. About 500 rhinos now live in Nepal, many of them guarded by armed soldiers in the Chitwan National Park.

Great Indian rhinos *are powerful animals with massive folds of skin that hang like sheets of armor plating. Their marshy grassland habitat provides them with the food, water, and shelter they need. The fertile soil is also ideal for farming, and the rhinos are being forced out. Major floods recently drowned many rhinos in areas near big rivers.*

The Indian government protects its rhinos, too. Nevertheless, in 1997, 25 were killed in the Kaziranga National Park alone. The park still contains over 1,000 rhinos, and it is feared that such a heavy concentration of animals could lead to disease. To reduce the risk of an epidemic sweeping through the population and inflicting heavy losses, it is important that in the future the animals are more widely dispersed. Conservationists could achieve this by reintroducing small populations to more distant areas.

29

Rhinoceros, Javan

Rhinoceros sondaicus

The Javan rhinoceros is currently the most endangered of the five rhinoceros species. A group of about 60 rhinos in an Indonesian national park may now be the only fairly safe population.

The Javan rhinoceros, like other species in the rhinoceros family, is characterized by its massive size, thick skin, and the single horn (actually made of a mass of compressed hairs) projecting from its nasal bone. Javan rhinos have a pointed, grasping upper lip, which is used to rip branches off bushes so that they can feed on the leaves. Sometimes they uproot small trees to get at their tender upper bark and foliage.

Javan rhinos are generally solitary. They normally stick to a familiar home patch, but may travel 10 miles (16 km) or more in a day to stay in another location for a while. The animals prefer lowland forests, but have been sighted on mountain slopes as high as 3,000 feet (900 m) above sea level, perhaps as a result of being driven from their usual haunts by disturbance and human settlement. They like the abundant cover provided by dense thickets and also favor wet regions offering the chance of wallowing in the mud in the steamy forest. Many such places have been cleared, drained, and developed by farmers, and the rich soil used to raise cattle and grow crops.

Another threat to the animals is the continuing demand for rhino horn in Eastern medicine. For centuries rhino horn has been thought to cure headaches and other disorders and to be an aphrodisiac. Like other rhinos, first in Asia and later in Africa too, the Javan species was shot, speared, and trapped by hunters, even though the males have only one small horn and the females often lack them. The Javan rhino's distribution has shrunk, and the population has become fragmented, so animals now stand less chance of finding an adequate selection of potential mates. The population is now genetically weakened as well as perilously small.

DATA PANEL

Javan rhinoceros

Rhinoceros sondaicus

Family: Rhinocerotidae

World population: Probably fewer than 80

Distribution: Indonesia (Java); also Vietnam and perhaps Cambodia or Laos

Habitat: Areas of reed, bamboo, and tall grasses in tropical forests and along rivers

Size: Length head/body: 10–10.5 ft (3–3.2 m); tail: 28 in (70 cm); height at shoulder: 5–5.8 ft (1.6–1.8 m); female larger than male. Weight: 3,200–4,400 lb (1,500–2,000 kg)

Form: Resembles an Indian rhino, but is more lightly built. The skin is less knobby, but hangs in similar platelike folds. There is a single horn, usually less than 6 in (15 cm) long

Diet: Leaves, bark, and twigs stripped from trees; also fallen fruit taken from the ground

Breeding: A single calf is born at 4–5 year intervals, after gestation of 16 months. It suckles for up to 2 years and takes 4–6 years to reach maturity. A life span of over 20 years is possible

Related endangered species: Sumatran rhinoceros (*Dicerorhinus sumatrensis*)* CR; black rhinoceros (*Diceros bicornis*)* CR; great Indian rhinoceros (*Rhinoceros unicornis*)* EN; white rhinoceros (*Ceratotherium simum*)* LRcd

Status: IUCN CR; CITES I

See also: CITES **1:** 12; Populations **1:** 20; Hunting **1:** 42; rhinoceros species **8:** 26–35

The Javan rhino, *unlike many badly reduced species, does not have the safety-net of a captive zoo population that could, if necessary, be reintroduced into the wild.*

Remnant Populations

At one time the Javan rhinoceros was found over much of Southeast Asia, but it is now extinct almost everywhere. The Javan rhino once lived in Vietnam, an area that was devastated by war in the 1970s, including heavy bombing and spraying of herbicide (Agent Orange) to kill the vegetation. This, and the enormous numbers of land mines left by the war, must have affected the rhino population badly. Nevertheless, in 1988 evidence was found of about 12 Javan rhinos still living north of Ho Chi Minh City.

For over half a century now the only significant population—about 50 to 60 rhinos—has lived in the Ujon Kulong National Park at the western end of Java. Even these animals are not completely safe, and they face natural threats such as disease and changes in the vegetation that make the habitat less suitable. There are no Javan rhinos in the world's zoos, and it is estimated that only nine have been kept in captivity.

There may still be a few individuals in southern Laos and Cambodia. As those countries recover after decades of war, more rhinos may be found. However, recovery may encourage rural development, leading to the extinction of any rhinos that remain there.

Rhinoceros, Sumatran

Dicerorhinus sumatrensis

The Sumatran rhinoceros closely resembles its ancestors that lived 40 million years ago. It is now on the brink of extinction; fewer than 1,000 individuals survive. Like other species of rhinoceros, it has suffered from hunting to obtain body parts for use in traditional medicines.

The small, hairy Sumatran rhinoceros lives deep in the forests of tropical Asia. Like other rhinos, it depends on water and is also very attracted to salt licks (places it can go to lick naturally occurring salt deposits). Unlike other species, it seems at home in mountain forests and can climb steep slopes surprisingly well. Indeed, some Sumatran rhinos may migrate to higher altitudes to avoid flooding in the rainy season or to escape the flies that plague them at certain times of year. The animals also avoid such pests by spending much of the day submerged in muddy wallows.

The Sumatran rhino can swim well and has even been seen in the sea. Normally active at night, it uses well-worn trails to travel through the forest and moves to a new feeding area every week or two to avoid running out of food; it eats about 100 pounds (45 kg) of leaves and shrubs every day. Males live alone and use a total range of about 12 square miles (30 sq. km). Females are more sedentary and are often seen in company with their single offspring, although otherwise they too live alone.

The Threat from Humans

Like other rhinos, the Sumatran rhino has been persecuted for its horns and other body parts, which are used in traditional oriental medicine. Habitat loss is also a problem since the wet lowlands where the animals live can be drained to create excellent farmland. With the ever-growing

DATA PANEL

Sumatran rhinoceros

Dicerorhinus sumatrensis

Family: Rhinocerotidae

World population: About 500–1,000

Distribution: Parts of Indonesia, Malaysia, Myanmar (Burma), Thailand, and Vietnam

Habitat: Forests, including hot lowland jungle and cool, wet moss forests in mountain regions

Size: Length: 7.8–10.5 ft (2.4–3.1 m); height at shoulder: 3.7–4.8 ft (1.1–1.5 m). Weight: 1,760–2,200 lb (800–1,000 kg)

Form: The smallest living rhinoceros, with 2 small, rounded horns. Gray-brown and distinctly hairy, especially younger animals

Diet: Woody vegetation, bark, leaves, twigs, vines, small shrubs. Also fruit such as mangoes and figs

Breeding: A single calf born after 13-month gestation. Independent at about 18 months, but takes up to 8 years to reach maturity. Births at intervals of 3–4 years. Has lived for up to 32 years in captivity

Related endangered species: Great Indian rhinoceros (*Rhinoceros unicornis*)* EN; Javan rhinoceros (*R. sondaicus*)* CR; black rhinoceros (*Diceros bicornis*)* CR; white rhinoceros (*Ceratotherium simum*)* LRcd

Status: IUCN CR; CITES I

See also: Biomes 1: 18; Hunting 1: 42; The History of Mammals 1: 60; rhinoceros species 8: 26–35

demand for land to feed Asia's burgeoning human population, the rhinos have been forced out of their natural homes. The problem is made worse by the fact that the Sumatran rhino likes to feed on secondary forest growth—the type of shrubs and trees that grow rapidly when natural forests are cleared. This preference unfortunately brings them into close contact with people and so increases their chances of being snared, trapped, or shot.

The Sumatran rhino has one natural advantage over other species: It is able to survive on steep slopes unsuitable for farming. However, even many areas of hilly forest have been felled for timber (especially in Malaysia) or to make room for oil palm plantations. Such activity not only deprives the rhinos of precious living space, but also necessitates road-building, making it easier for poachers to penetrate remote areas and leaving nowhere for the rhinos to hide. As a result, it is likely that the species is already extinct in Cambodia. It was long believed to have

died out in India too, the last animals supposedly having been seen there in 1967. However, a survey of India's border with Myanmar (Burma) in 1996 revealed signs that a few Sumatran rhinos might have survived. The uncertainty stems from the fact that the animal is remarkably hard to detect. In 1991 it was rediscovered in a part of Sumatra where it was thought to have died out over 30 years before, and it also turned up unexpectedly in Sarawak in 1987, having been considered extinct there for 40 years. There may be a few in Laos, Cambodia, or Vietnam. A few Sumatran rhinos are held in zoos and in fenced protected areas in Indonesia.

The smallest living rhino, *the Sumatran rhino is the only survivor of a group that includes the now extinct woolly rhinoceros. Shy forest-dwellers, the animals have a distinctive hairy coat.*

Rhinoceros, White

Ceratotherium simum

Like other species of rhinoceros, the white rhino has been threatened by hunting and habitat loss, but it has also been declining naturally for centuries.

The white rhinoceros is one of the largest of all living land animals. It normally lives alone or in small groups, remaining in much the same area for long periods and occupying an unusually small home range for such a large animal, typically of up to about 3 square miles (8 sq. km). White rhinos are generally placid creatures and can be approached easily. Consequently, they are vulnerable to attack by humans, although they have little to fear from other predators because of their massive size.

Fossils, bones, and ancient rock paintings suggest that the white rhino was once widespread across most of Africa, including part of what is now the Sahara Desert. Even in historic times it ranged as far north and west as the shores of Lake Chad. However, the most serious decline in white rhino numbers occurred long before the modern pressures of hunting and habitat loss that have brought its cousin, the black rhino, to the brink of extinction. By the beginning of the 20th century the white rhino was reduced to a couple of remnant populations: A few individuals survived in South Africa, and there was a tiny group on the borders of what was then Zaire (now the Democratic Republic of Congo), Uganda, and the Sudan, forming a separate northern subspecies.

Exactly why the white rhino should have declined so much in its distributional range is something of a mystery. Perhaps the problem was that it feeds on short grass and therefore comes into competition with the many other animals, such as gazelles and zebras, that graze the same habitat. As they became more numerous, the rhinos may have found foraging more difficult. The white rhino needs to be close to water; if local waterholes dry up in the absence of rain, many

rhinos perish. The rhino is therefore particularly susceptible to the effects of drought, a frequent occurrence in many parts of Africa.

Mixed Fortunes

As the white rhino rapidly approached extinction—at one point the southern population had shrunk to fewer than two dozen animals—careful conservation measures were put in place for the species' protection. Slowly the numbers increased; today there are probably about 5,000 white rhinos widely distributed across southern Africa. They are now relatively safe, being found only in national parks and reserves, where they are protected from poachers and have plenty of suitable habitat. For this reason the species is currently classified by the IUCN as Low Risk, Conservation Dependent and is regarded as secure.

However, the northern white rhinos have not fared so well. The small northern population occurs in an area of great human poverty, where resources are simply not available to mount effective conservation programs or to ensure protection from poaching and

See also: CITES **1:** 12; Hunting **1:** 42; rhinoceros species **8:** 26–33

habitat destruction. Recent wars in the area have made guns widely available, and strong economic pressures exist to encourage poaching and the sale of the valuable horns. Probably fewer than 50 animals remain, most of them in a single national park in the Democratic Republic of Congo.

In addition to the survivors in the wild, there are about 120 white rhinos held in 40 zoos around the world, but they have not bred well. In particular, the four northern white rhinos in captivity have failed to reproduce and are now getting too old to do so.

The white rhino *is actually gray or brownish in color and is often stained by mud or dust. It has a broad, straight upper lip 8 inches (20 cm) wide, which is used for cropping short grass.*

DATA PANEL

White rhinoceros

Ceratotherium simum

Family: Rhinocerotidae

World population: About 5,000

Distribution: The Sudan-Uganda-Democratic Republic of Congo border; parts of South Africa

Habitat: Short-grass areas of savanna

Size: Length: 11.8–13.8 ft (3.6–4.2 m); tail: 31–39 in (80–100 cm); height at shoulder: 5.6–6.1 ft (1.7–1.9 m). Weight: 3,080–4,400 lb (1,400–2,000 kg); up to 7,920 lb (3,600 kg)

Form: A large rhinoceros; gray (but often discolored by mud or dust) with 2 horns. Mouth broad; upper lip very wide

Diet: Short grasses; sometimes new growth after fires

Breeding: Single calf born after 16-month gestation; males mature at 10 years, females at 6–7 years. Life span may exceed 30 years

Related endangered species: Black rhinoceros (*Diceros bicornis*)* CR; Great Indian rhinoceros (*Rhinoceros unicornis*)* EN; Javan rhinoceros (*R. sondaicus*)* CR; Sumatran rhinoceros (*Dicerorhinus sumatrensis*)* CR

Status: IUCN LRcd; northen population CITES I, southern CITES II

Rock-Wallaby, Prosperine

Petrogale persephone

A recent addition to the Australian list of scientifically described mammal species, the Prosperine rock-wallaby is in danger of disappearing before it has been fully studied. However, in this particular case of endangerment it seems that people are not entirely to blame.

The Prosperine rock-wallaby—so-named because it was found close to the town of Prosperine—has the most restricted distribution of any rock-wallaby species. Today's population appears to be all that remains of a once widespread animal. Well before people began making scientific observations of Australian wildlife, it had undergone a drastic population decline. It seems that gradual changes in climate and vegetation since the Pleistocene era (two million years ago) have not suited the species, and it has been edged out of most of its former range by two better-adapted forms: the unadorned rock-wallaby and the yellow-footed rock-wallaby. It is unfortunate for the Prosperine rock-wallaby that its last refuge happens to be in one of the fastest-developing regions of Australia.

Amazingly, given that the population lives so close to large human settlements, the Prosperine rock-wallaby was not officially recognized until 1976. Local people were aware that the wallabies existed before then, but the species is very shy and retiring, and few scientists ever got more than a fleeting glimpse as the wallabies melted into the forest or slipped quickly and quietly away over the rocks.

Habitat Pressures

Since the Prosperine rock-wallaby was formally described, a big effort has been made to study its habitat and distribution. The results are not encouraging. The populations on the mainland are small and isolated, living on tiny patches of habitat surrounded by urban development, agricultural land, or roads. This part of the Queensland coast is a rapidly expanding tourist destination. Since most of the Prosperine

DATA PANEL	
Prosperine rock-wallaby ***Petrogale persephone*** **Family:** Macropodidae **World population:** Unknown **Distribution:** Northeastern Queensland and Whitsunday Islands, Australia **Habitat:** Deciduous coastal forests with grassy areas and rocky outcrops **Size:** Length head/body: 19.5–25 in (50–64 cm); tail: 20–27 in (51–68 cm); male up to 50% larger than female. Weight: 9–20 lb (4–9 kg)	**Form:** Dog-sized animal with dark-gray fur tinged with red in places, especially around ears, face, and shoulders; white fur on chin blends with pale underside; feet and tail strikingly black **Diet:** Grasses **Breeding:** Single young born at any time of year; further details unknown **Related endangered species:** At least 16 other species of wallaby and kangaroo, including Goodfellow's tree kangaroo (*Dendrolagus goodfellowi*)* EN **Status:** IUCN EN; not listed by CITES

See also: Natural Extinction **1:** 34; Tourism **1:** 42; Tree-Kangaroo, Goodfellow's **10:** 4

rock-wallaby's habitat is in private hands, there is little to stop it being developed one fragment at a time. It is a sad fact that most close encounters between people and Prosperine rock-wallabies are when the animals are killed in road accidents.

The Prosperine rock-wallaby is larger than most of its close relatives, but still small enough to be vulnerable to attack by dingoes and larger domestic or feral (wild) dogs. Domestic cats may also pose a threat, not because they hunt the wallabies, but because they carry a disease called toxoplasmosis, which may affect wallabies as well. The combined effect of the threats, added to the original problem of competition with other wallaby species, adds up to a grim outlook for the Prosperine rock-wallaby, especially on the Australian mainland.

There are, however, small additional populations of the endangered Prosperine rock-wallaby on several nearby islands, some of which—including Dryander, Conway, and Gloucester Islands—are national parks. While the colonies are still highly vulnerable on account of their small size, the islands are free of predators and protected from development. It seems that the islands will soon provide the only secure refuge for the species, which may otherwise be destined for extinction in the wild.

In the future the small wild populations on the mainland and the various island refuges could be boosted by the reintroduction of captive-bred individuals. The wallabies could in time be relocated to other island habitats from which predators and competing species have been removed. Such intervention may give the species a fighting chance.

The Prosperine rock-wallaby *is larger than most of its closely related competitors. Even so, it seems to have been losing the battle for habitat gradually over several thousand years.*

Rockfowl, White-Necked

Picathartes gymnocephalus

A curious-looking West African bird, the white-necked rockfowl owes its name to its habit of building nests in caves or among large boulders. It is seriously threatened by forest clearance and hunting, and most of its remaining breeding populations are tiny and fragmented.

The white-necked rockfowl is an odd-looking bird, and its habits are in some respects as unusual as its appearance. It has only one close relative: the gray-necked rockfowl, an equally threatened species with a range to the west of its own. The relationship that the two bear to other birds has long been controversial, with some researchers suggesting that they may share a common ancestry with crows or starlings; more recently, however, they have been linked to the babblers instead.

Whatever its past kinship, the rockfowl remains an unforgettable sight for the relatively few people lucky enough to have seen it. It bounds across the forest floor with curious, springy hops, using its long tail to keep its balance. The birds favor forest habitat in hilly lowland areas, seeking out steep slopes for their nesting sites. They breed in colonies of up to 40 pairs. The nests are often set under towering cliffs, either beneath overhangs or else in shallow caverns, since the rockfowl is one of only a few bird species to nest (and roost) in caves. On occasion pairs have also been found nesting inside fallen tree trunks.

Staying Close to Home

Rockfowl have rarely been recorded far from their breeding sites, where they forage for large insects and other prey found on or close to the forest floor. They explore moss-carpeted boulders, tangled creepers, and the roots and lower growths of giant trees festooned with hanging moss and lianas. They can sometimes be seen along the banks of streams, tossing leaves aside with their bills as they hunt for food. Together with bristlebills, alethes, and Finsch's flycatcher-thrushes, rockfowl have often been observed feeding on insects fleeing from swarms of army ants.

On the ground the birds' hopping progress is interrupted with pauses in which they crane their necks to peer through the darkness of the forest. They sometimes use their broad, rounded wings to make brief, low-level flights among the tree trunks, but rarely fly far. Although usually wary, rockfowl can be inquisitive on occasion, deliberately drawing near intruders in order to get a closer look.

DATA PANEL

White-necked rockfowl (white-necked picathartes, bare-headed rockfowl)

Picathartes gymnocephalus

Family: Picathartidae

World population: Estimated at 2,500–10,000 birds

Distribution: Parts of Guinea, Sierra Leone, Liberia, Ivory Coast, and Ghana

Habitat: Primary and mature secondary forest, gallery forest, and forest clearings in hilly, rocky country

Size: Length: 15–16 in (38–41 cm). Weight: 5.5–8 oz (160–225 g)

Form: Pigeon-sized bird with long neck and strongly patterned, naked head. Long, curving tail; long, powerful legs; head bright yellow apart from black patches behind each eye; strong, black bill; nape has short, silky white feathers forming wispy ruff; sturdy, gray-blue legs and feet

Diet: Chiefly insects, including cockroach larvae, earwigs, beetles, ants, and termites; also centipedes, millipedes, earthworms, snails, and small crustaceans, lizards and frogs

Breeding: Nests sited on walls or roofs of caves, on rock faces, cliffs, or large boulders; occasionally in large, fallen, hollow trees; nest is deep, thick-walled cup of mud, vegetable fibers, and rootlets; usually 2 cream, pale-gray, or dark-fawn eggs, blotched or mottled brown or gray; incubation 3–4 weeks; fledging 3–4 weeks

Related endangered species: Gray-necked rockfowl (*Picathartes oreas*) VU

Status: IUCN VU; CITES I

See also: War 1: 47; Education 1: 94; Swallow, Blue 9: 42

The white-necked rockfowl spends much of its time on or near the ground, rarely straying far from its nesting sites.

An Uncertain Future

Restricted by its specific habitat needs, the white-necked rockfowl is certainly more scarce and less widespread today than it was in the past. In Ghana, for instance, there were many records of breeding colonies until the 1960s, but there have been no confirmed reports since then. Throughout its range the bird has suffered from forest clearance for timber and mining or else to make way for rice cultivation. The rate of destruction has been particularly great over the last two decades.

In Liberia the situation has been made worse by uncontrolled logging undertaken to pay for weapons and troops for use in the country's recent civil war. In Sierra Leone traditional nesting sites have been abandoned not only where forest has been felled, but also where it has become degraded; human disturbance at some locations has been found to significantly reduce breeding success. Another threat comes from trapping; local people sometimes snare the birds for food or else catch them on their nests at night by torchlight. As the amount of available habitat shrinks, competition for nest sites grows, and in addition, predators take some eggs.

Until only about 10 years ago rockfowl used to be captured for the zoo trade; in Liberia many colonies were wiped out as a result. Many of the birds that were taken died within a day of being captured. Although some chicks were bred successfully, attempts to establish a viable captive-breeding program failed.

A working group has recently been set up to protect the species and to halt its continuing decline. One of the first priorities conservationists have set themselves is to carry out surveys to establish current population levels—or, in Ghana, to see if any birds survive at all. Other targets include monitoring populations and mobilizing the support of local people to protect large colonies of the birds.

In the 1990s both white- and gray-necked rockfowl became important symbols for the promotion of bird conservation and responsible ecotourism in the West African rain forest. It is to be hoped that the birds can be saved so that future generations can learn more about their mysterious lives.

Rocky, Eastern Province

Sandelia bainsii

Most fish rely exclusively on their gills to breathe. Some use their guts as auxiliary (or secondary) respiratory organs, taking gulps of air at the surface of the water. Yet others—called labyrinth fish— use a special organ located within the skull to help them survive in oxygen-deficient or poor-quality water. The eastern province rocky has such an organ, but it still faces extinction.

There has been growing concern for the eastern province rocky for well over a decade. It is not a widespread species, being restricted to the Eastern Cape in South Africa, where it is known to occur only in a handful of tributaries and pools. Such a situation places any species under pressure.

With its supplementary respiratory organ called a labyrinth that allows it to breathe atmospheric air, the eastern province rocky should stand a reasonable chance of survival where water quality is poor. However, the fish has evolved under environmental conditions that are more oxygen-rich than those encountered by its close relatives, the *Anabas* and *Ctenopoma* species; its preferred habitat is flowing waters rather than swamps. As a result, it has evolved under reduced natural selection pressure for the development of an efficient labyrinth.

Invasion of Habitat

With its reduced capacity for breathing air, the eastern province rocky's survival is threatened. It is not only the drop in water quality and the associated reduction in oxygen levels that has been a major factor in the rocky's demise; damming has also played its part, along with water extraction and the introduction of nonnative fish and plant species. Among the introduced fish *Tilapia* are outcompeting native species in their struggle for space and food, while predators like bass and the sharptooth catfish are also taking their toll on eastern province rocky numbers.

DATA PANEL

Eastern province rocky

Sandelia bainsii

Family: Anabantidae

World population: Low in most locations; close to extinction in others

Distribution: Eastern Cape, South Africa; tributaries of Buffalo, Great Fish, Keiskamma, and Kowie river systems; a small population has also been confirmed in the Nahoon River

Habitat: Rocky streams and pools, usually with wedges, rocks, or other submerged objects that provide shelter. Juveniles often found in shallow areas around pool edges

Size: Length: about 10 in (25 cm); male up to 12.8 in (32.5 cm); female smaller

Form: Chunky body with large head and mouth. Pointed dorsal (back) and anal (belly) fin in male, with small extensions to fin rays of caudal (tail). Base color of body is blue-gray, fading to lighter shades toward abdomen; occasionally has greeny-yellow sheen; coloration may vary with locality

Diet: Small fish, insects, and aquatic invertebrates

Breeding: Male turns black with blue-purple tinge, contrasting sharply with white dorsal, anal, and caudal fin edges. Unlike many other labyrinth fish, male does not build bubble nest. Instead, it clears small area on bottom over which spawning pair embrace and releases up to 7,000 adhesive, sinking eggs. Male guards eggs until they hatch some 2 days later at 72–74°F (22–23°C)

Related endangered species: None

Status: IUCN EN; not listed by CITES

See also: Specialization 1: 28; Introductions 1: 54; Caracolera, Mojarra 3: 26; Darter, Watercress 4: 4

Of the introduced plant species the aquatic South American fairy fern has proved to be the greatest menace, covering large sections of the eastern province rocky's habitat in an unbroken green "blanket." The fairy fern is having a devastating effect on the fish's environment. Its impenetrable fronds prevent sunlight from reaching submerged vegetation, which, like all other types of vegetation, relies on the availability of sunlight for photosynthesis, a by-product of which is oxygen. A reduced rate of photosynthesis means that less dissolved oxygen in the water is available for aquatic animals.

The South American fairy fern is also having a dramatic effect on water temperature in the streams and pools inhabited by the eastern province rocky. In deep sections of water the shade it produces lowers the water temperature. In shallow areas the fern absorbs heat from the sun, thereby raising the temperature. For the young eastern province rockies the fairy fern presents yet another obstacle to survival: Juvenile fish can become stranded among the dense fronds, unable to return to clear water.

The eastern province rocky has benefited from such measures as the removal of the South American fairy fern from its habitat and the release of captive-bred stock.

Saving the Rocky

Attempts to save the eastern province rocky from extinction have been underway for 10 years. Support has come from many sources, including hobby organizations, individuals, and industry. The need for support continues since the tasks facing the Eastern Province Rocky Conservation Project are immense. Loss of habitat still occurs as a result of deforestation and overgrazing (causing silting), while damming and other forms of river management can fragment populations and introduce nonnative species. In addition, careless use of local streams introduces detergents and other pollutants. The campaign—including the establishment of the Blaauwkrantz Nature Reserve to protect the species—is undoubtedly having some success. Public awareness of the problem is also increasing.

Saiga

Saiga tatarica

By the early 20th century uncontrolled hunting had brought the saiga antelope to the brink of extinction. Despite efforts to protect the species, it is still at risk from poaching.

The saiga is a curious-looking mammal. It is physically well adapted to the dry, dusty open plains of southern Russia and Mongolia where it lives. One of its most distinguishing features is its large nose, which inflates to allow the cold air it breathes in to be warmed. The nose also acts as an effective dust filter.

Saigas live in large, wandering herds. Those living west of the Caspian Sea undertake seasonal migrations in the spring and fall, traveling an amazing 50 to 75 miles (80 to 120 km) a day and with a total range of 9,650 square miles (25,000 sq. km). The animals spend the summer in herds of only a few dozen. In the fall large groups form for the migration south. During November the males attempt to defend harems of up to 15 females and to mate with them. When spring arrives, the males form herds of up to 2,000 animals and travel back to the summer feeding grounds. The females follow in vast herds of 100,000 or more, spreading over a huge area. On this journey they may stop briefly to have their young.

Uncontrolled Hunting

In the Pleistocene epoch (between 10,000 and 1,700,000 years ago) the saiga was found from Britain all across northern Europe and Russia to Alaska. As the climate warmed at the end of the last ice age, the saiga retreated to the wild open steppes of Central Asia. Here it became prey to both wolves and humans. Saigas were prized for their meat and skins. The horns too were highly valued in Eastern medicine since they were believed to have medicinal properties. The animals were hunted on horseback and sometimes driven onto long barriers of sharpened stakes on which they were killed in great numbers. By the early 20th century this uncontrolled killing had reduced the saiga population to about 1,000 animals.

Temporary Recovery

At this point the Soviet Union took action, and populations recovered to an estimated 2 million. By 1958 huge herds once again roamed the Central Asian grasslands, producing an annual harvest of skins, meat, and horns. Numbers were carefully monitored, and only selected animals were allowed to be killed. In saiga herds only a small fraction of the males manage to hold a harem and breed. Surplus

See also: Biomes **1:** 18; Hunting **1:** 42; Antelope, Tibetan **2:** 26

Saiga

Saiga tatarica

Family: Bovidae

World population: Probably fewer than 1 million

Distribution: Central Asia: Kazakhstan, Mongolia, and Kalmykia

Habitat: Arid grassland plains

Size: Length: 42–54 in (100–140 cm); height at shoulder: 24–30 in (60–75 cm). Weight: 45–112 lb (20–50 kg)

Form: Goat-sized mammal. Pale brown in summer with sparse, bristly hair; coat almost white in winter, becoming long and thick. Nose large, bulging, and inflatable. Horns (males only) are semitransparent, 8–10 in (20–25 cm) long, and almost vertical

Diet: Mainly grass; over 100 other small plants and shrubs found growing on the steppes

Breeding: Females can breed from 6 months (males 2 years); twins born March–early April after 5-month gestation. Young nursed by their mothers for up to 4 months. Life span up to 10 years

Related endangered species: No close relatives

Status: IUCN LRcd; CITES II

males were therefore harvested, leaving more food for the females and their young. As a result of this and other measures, survival rates continued to rise until about 1990.

Uncertain Future

Following the breakup of the Soviet Union, poaching is no longer controlled, and the careful management of herds is in jeopardy. Although there are a few saiga antelopes in zoos, there is no formal recovery program for the species.

Saigas *live in large herds. They normally graze in the early morning and evening and rest in the middle of the day. When fleeing, the animals can reach speeds of 50 miles per hour (80 km/h).*

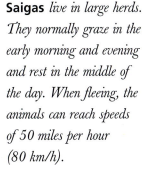

Salamander, California Tiger

Ambystoma californiense

Only recently recognized as a distinct species, the California tiger salamander is threatened by the destruction and fragmentation of its habitat.

The California tiger salamander leads a secretive life, spending most of its time underground in the burrows of ground squirrels, pocket gophers, and other burrowing animals. Described as an "explosive breeder," it emerges in large numbers after heavy rains in late winter and early spring, making mass migrations between November and April to temporary, rain-filled ponds.

Unpredictable Breeding Patterns

The California tiger salamander is well adapted to the unpredictable conditions of its habitat. It is a long-lived animal that is capable of producing large numbers of young when it gets the opportunity to breed—after heavy winter rain. Its breeding is therefore highly erratic. In a study of one population over 1,200 salamanders were born in one year and only three in another. The timing of breeding migrations also varies from year to year, depending on when the winter rains fall. In some years when there is little or no rain, the salamanders do not breed.

The male has a slightly longer tail than the female, and in the breeding season he develops a swollen cloaca (chamber into which the reproductive and digestive systems open). The salamander prefers to breed in ponds that are not inhabited by other amphibians. It is vital that its breeding ponds do not contain fish, since they would prey on the eggs and larvae, so it breeds only in ponds that appear with heavy rainfall and then drain away. Such a strategy is risky, since a pond may dry out before the larvae have matured. The eggs are laid singly or in small clutches and are attached to submerged vegetation. Larvae are yellow or gray in color with wide, flattened heads. They take between three and six months to complete their development.

Breeding populations typically contain many more males than females; males often outnumber females by two to one, sometimes by more. Courtship begins when a male approaches a female and nudges her with his snout. He then tries to lead her away, nudging her repeatedly with his tail. If she follows him, he stops and deposits a package of sperm, called a spermatophore, onto the bottom of the pond. He

DATA PANEL

California tiger salamander

Ambystoma californiense

Family: Ambystomatidae

World population: Unknown

Distribution: Central and western California

Habitat: Grassland and low hills with vernal pools (pools that occur in spring)

Size: Length: 6–8.5 in (15–22 cm)

Form: Stocky body with 12 grooves; broad, rounded snout; protruding eyes; back and sides black with pale-yellow spots; gray belly

Diet: Small aquatic invertebrates

Breeding: November–April; eggs laid singly or in small clutches; hatching period 2–4 weeks

Related endangered species: Flatwood salamander (*Ambystoma cingulatum*) VU; Lake Lerma salamander (*A. lermaense*) CR; axolotl (*A. mexicanum*)* VU

Status: IUCN VU; not listed by CITES

See also: Boom and Bust **1:** 21; Communities and Ecosystems **1:** 22; Salamander, Santa Cruz Long-Toed **8:** 50

The California tiger salamander *was classified as a distinct species in 1996, having previously been regarded as a subspecies of the tiger salamander.*

then moves away, and the female follows, stopping when her cloaca touches the spermatophore. She then squats on the spermatophore and takes up the sperm into her cloaca. Males are very active during the brief mating period and can deposit between eight and 37 spermatophores in a single night. They compete for access to females. A rival male can interfere with the activities of another male by positioning himself between a mating pair and mimicking the female's behavior. This causes the mating male to deposit a spermatophore; the rival then places a spermataphore of his own on top of it.

Habitat Destruction

The California tiger salamander has disappeared from much of its former range, primarily because its habitat has been destroyed to create space for housing and industrial development. It has also been adversely affected by campaigns to wipe out ground squirrels in built-up areas. People regard ground squirrels as pests,

but their burrows provide vital underground habitat for the California tiger salamanders. Fragmentation of the salamanders' habitat is as significant a problem as habitat loss. While substantial areas of suitable habitat are left— and some of them are protected—they are becoming isolated from one another by human development. As salamander populations become separated, there is little or no interchange of animals. Small populations suffer from inbreeding, gradually losing the genetic variation in the group that is vital if they are to adapt to long-term changes in their environment.

No one knows how far the California tiger salamander moves from its breeding pond between breeding seasons, either as a newly metamorphosed juvenile or as an adult. Effective conservation requires protection of both its breeding ponds and the land habitat where it spends most of its life. However, conservation efforts are impeded by the lack of knowledge about its range.

Salamander, Japanese Giant

Andrias japonicus

Restricted to just two mountainous areas, the Japanese giant salamander's mountain stream habitat is under threat from damming and deforestation. Collection has also depleted numbers. Fortunately, the salamander is now fully protected by international trade restrictions.

The Japanese giant salamander and its close relative the Chinese giant salamander from China and Taiwan are the largest salamanders in the world. An inhabitant of mountain streams with clear, cool water, the Japanese giant salamander is similar in anatomy and habits to the hellbender of North America, and the two Asian species are sometimes known as Oriental hellbenders.

The Japanese giant salamander has a heavily built, slightly compressed body and a flat head, with small eyes and nostrils at the tip of its snout. Its skin is rough and warty, with many wrinkles and folds, giving the impression that its body is too small for its skin. Two prominent folds run along the whole length of its body. The tail, which makes up about a quarter of its total length, is flattened from side to side and has a fin along the upper side. The limbs are small and also slightly flattened. In color the salamander is reddish or grayish brown with a darker mottled pattern, and it is paler on the underside. Males and females are similar in size and appearance, except that the male develops a swollen cloaca (cavity into which the alimentary canal, genital, and urinary ducts open) during the breeding season.

The Japanese giant salamander is a retiring animal by day, hiding under rocks or in a burrow. It emerges at night in search of food, which includes fish, worms, and crustaceans such as crayfish. It has an unusual arrangement of jawbones and muscles, which enables it to suck its prey into its mouth. It requires the clean, well-oxygenated water that is found only in fast-flowing streams and so is confined to altitudes between 980 and 3,300 feet (300 and 1,000 m). The Chinese giant salamander is found in a similar habitat, but also occurs in mountain lakes.

Breathing through the Skin

The giant salamanders show a form of pedomorphosis, retaining many aspects of the larval form into adult life. Unlike some pedomorphic salamanders, however, giant salamanders lose their external gills when they are about 18 months old and about 4.5 inches (12 cm) in length. Thereafter they rely on their skin to absorb oxygen from the water. The skin of giant salamanders contains a higher density of blood capillaries than most

DATA PANEL

Japanese giant salamander

Andrias japonicus

Family: Cryptobranchidae

World population: Unknown

Distribution: Southern Japan; islands of Honshu and Kyushu

Habitat: Rocky mountain streams with clear, fast-flowing, and well-oxygenated water

Size: Length: 8–56 in (20–140 cm)

Form: Large salamander; long, flattened body; rough, warty skin with many wrinkles and folds. Laterally compressed tail with dorsal (back) fin. Broad, flat head; small eyes. Reddish or grayish brown on upper body; paler below

Diet: Fish, worms, and crustaceans

Breeding: Fall (August–September)

Related endangered species: Chinese giant salamander *(Andrias davidianus)* DD

Status: IUCN VU; CITES I

salamanders, and the many wrinkles and folds in the skin increase the surface area over which oxygen is absorbed. When resting, the salamanders sway slowly from side to side; this serves to gently stir up the water, ensuring that well-oxygenated water is always close to their skin.

Paternal Care

Breeding begins in the fall (August to September). The male Japanese giant salamander plays a more active role than is true for most salamanders. He digs a pit in the gravel on a stream bed, defending his territory aggressively against rival males. At the same time, he displays to attract a female into the pit. The female lays 400 to 600 eggs in strings that are between 7 and 60 feet (2 and 18 m) in length, and the male sheds sperm onto them. Mating attracts the attention of other, usually smaller males, who enter the nest and also shed sperm on the eggs. After mating, the female leaves the male, who guards the eggs until they hatch, after about two months. The newly hatched larvae disperse from the nest and reach maturity at about three years of age. Giant salamanders are very long-lived; one animal, in Amsterdam Zoo, lived to be 52 years old.

Protected Species

The large size of the Japanese giant salamander, together with its specific habitat requirements, means that it was never an abundant creature. As a result, it has been particularly badly affected by deforestation and the damming of rivers, activities that destroy the clear, well-oxygenated streams it prefers.

Japanese giant salamanders have also been collected in the past and sent to many museums, aquaria, and zoos throughout the world. However, this kind of trade is now tightly controlled, the species having been given full protection under the CITES treaty.

The Japanese giant salamander *loses its external gills at about 18 months, when it is about 4.5 inches (12 cm) in length.*

Salamander, Ouachita Red-Backed

Plethodon serratus

Representative of a number of rare North American salamanders, the Ouachita red-backed salamander is threatened by the degradation and loss of its woodland habitat.

The Ouachita red-backed salamander gets its name from the Ouachita Mountains of Arkansas and Oklahoma; its "red back" refers to the orange or red stripe that runs down the length of its body and tail. The edges resemble the edge of a saw, with "teeth" corresponding to the costal grooves that run around the salamander's body.

The animal was recognized as a species in 1975, having been regarded as a subspecies of the red-backed salamander. It is one of a small group of closely related species, many of which are threatened.

The plethodontid salamanders are the largest and most diverse family of tailed amphibians and the only group to be found in tropical habitats. They are remarkable for lacking lungs; it is believed that their ancestors evolved a lungless condition because they lived in cool mountain streams where the high oxygen content of the water made it possible for them to get all the oxygen they needed through their skin. Many modern plethodontids are terrestrial animals, without the need to be close to streams or ponds, but they are generally active only in cool, damp weather. They are small animals that have minimal food requirements, an occasional meal being enough to maintain their low metabolism and to sustain a slow rate of growth. As a result, plethodontid salamanders can be found in large numbers in suitable habitats.

On the Forest Floor

The red-backed salamanders are wholly terrestrial in their habitat, living in deep leaf litter on the floor of hardwood forests where there is plenty of cover provided by rocks and fallen logs. For much of the time they live in burrows in the ground, emerging on cool, damp nights to forage on the surface for ants, beetles, and other insect prey. They stay inactive in summer when it is too dry to come out and during cold spells in winter.

The Ouachita red-backed salamander's range is unusual, being

DATA PANEL

Ouachita red-backed salamander (Southern red-backed salamander)

Plethodon serratus

Family: Plethodontidae

World population: Unknown

Distribution: Four separate areas in southeastern U.S.

Habitat: Hardwood forests

Size: Length: 2.7–4 in (7–10 cm)

Form: Small, slender salamander with 18 or 19 costal grooves. Gray or black with a tooth-edged orange or red stripe down the middle of the back

Diet: Small invertebrates, especially ants and beetles

Breeding: December–March, depending on locality. Females breed biennially, males annually

Related endangered species: Peaks of Otter salamander (*Plethodon hubrichti*) VU; Cheat Mountain salamander (*P. nettingi*) VU; Shenandoah salamander (*P. shenandoah*) EN; Siskiyou Mountains salamander (*P. stormi*) VU

Status: Not listed by IUCN; not listed by CITES

See also: Communities and Ecosystems 1: 22; salamander species 8: 44–51

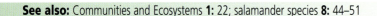

divided into four
distinct and isolated areas:
the Salem Mountains of Missouri;
the Ouachita Mountains of Arkansas and
Oklahoma; the Piedmont and Blue Ridge Mountains of
Georgia, Alabama, and Tennessee; and central
Louisiana. The salamanders are found at altitudes of
up to 5,500 feet (1,700 m), and the timing of
breeding varies from one part of their range to
another. Courtship and mating occur in December in
the Blue Ridge Mountains, in February and March in
Georgia, and between December and March in
Missouri. In May or June females lay a small clutch of
four to 10 large eggs in underground burrows; they
stay with them, guarding the eggs against predators
and cleaning off any fungal infestation. The eggs
hatch into young—miniature versions of the adults—in
July or August.

Despite their small clutch, the energetic cost of
egg production for females is apparently very high.
They breed only every other year, while the males
breed every year.

Habitat Loss

The Ouachita red-backed salamander and several of its
close relatives are threatened by habitat loss. The
woodland that they inhabit is highly prized for its

The Ouachita red-backed salamander *is a member of
the remarkable plethodontid salamander family, which lacks
lungs. Plethodontids absorb oxygen through their skin.*

timber, and tree felling eliminates the shade that
provides a cool, damp environment. Able to breathe
only through their.skin, plethodontid salamanders
cannot survive in warm, dry air. Exploitation of the
forest also reduces the amount of leaf litter that is
available for cover and that also supports their prey. In
addition, the forests of the central and eastern United
States have been affected by acid rain.

Confined Ranges

Not all members of the family Plethodontidae have
small ranges. The red-backed salamander, for example,
can be found across eastern North America. However,
the Ouachita red-backed salamander and its close
relatives are confined to small areas. The Ouachita is
found in only one or a few small mountain ranges,
while another family member, the Shenandoah
salamander, inhabits a small area between the
altitudes of 3,000 and 3,750 feet (914 and 1,143 m)
in northeastern Virginia. The Ouachita red-backed
salamander is prone to extinction simply because
deforestation or any kind of habitat change is likely to
affect its entire range.

Salamander, Santa Cruz Long-Toed

Ambystoma macrodactylum croceum

The Santa Cruz long-toed salamander lives in small areas of Monterey Bay, California. It is threatened by the loss of its restricted habitat.

The Santa Cruz long-toed salamander is a subspecies of the long-toed salamander, which has an extensive range, running from California in the south to British Columbia in the north and eastward to Alberta and Montana. At some point in the distant past the Santa Cruz population became isolated from the rest of the species' range, and it is now confined to a few areas in Monterey Bay, California. The species as a whole remains relatively common, but the Santa Cruz subspecies has become extremely rare.

Spring Breeder

One of the first amphibians to breed in the spring, the Santa Cruz long-toed salamander sometimes begins to migrate to its breeding sites as early as October, but more usually in January or February. It reacts immediately when heavy rains fill up the breeding ponds and is an example of an "explosive breeder." Breeding is concluded quickly, with mating and egg-laying completed in just a week. Males migrate to

water just before females. The sexes are similar in size and appearance, except that the male has slightly longer limbs and tail, and a swollen cloaca (cavity into which the alimentary canal, genital, and urinary ducts open). It contains a complex array of glands that make spermatophores, the capsules in which sperm are transferred to females.

The breeding season is brief and does not allow males time to set up territories. Instead, they wander around the pond in search of females. On finding one, the male clasps her, wrapping his forelimbs around her body, and rubs the glands under his chin on her head. This chin-rubbing becomes more intense until the male dismounts, sliding forward over her head, and takes up a position in front of her. He raises and waves his tail, and the female moves forward to nudge the base of his tail or cloaca with her snout. He then deposits a

Oregon | Idaho
Nevada | Utah | Colorado
UNITED STATES
California | Arizona | New Mexico
MEXICO

DATA PANEL

Santa Cruz long-toed salamander

Ambystoma macrodactylum croceum

Family: Ambystomatidae

World population: Unknown

Distribution: A few areas in Monterey County, California

Habitat: Ponds during the breeding season; otherwise among rotting vegetation and under logs near ponds

Size: Length: 4–6.8 in (10–17 cm)

Form: Slender body with long tail; 12 or 13 costal

grooves (grooves around the body that conduct water from the ground to the upper parts of the body); glossy black skin with yellow or orange stripe or spots; white speckles on flanks; underside gray or black

Diet: Small invertebrates

Breeding: Occurs in late winter or early spring. Male deposits spermatophore; fertilization is internal in female; eggs develop into larvae in pond

Related endangered species: California tiger salamander (*Ambystoma californiense*)* VU; axolotl (*A. mexicanum*)* VU

Status: Not listed by IUCN; not listed by CITES

See also: Natural Disasters **1:** 57; Saving the Habitats **1:** 88; salamander species **8:** 44–49

spermatophore, which has a mass of sperm on top of it. The female moves over the spermatophore, removing the sperm mass with her open cloaca.

One sperm mass is usually sufficient to fertilize a female's eggs, but males are capable of producing them in large numbers: Individual males have been observed to produce up to 15 spermatophores in five hours. This high level of productivity offsets the fact that sperm transfer is by an unreliable method—many spermatophores are missed by females—but it also means that one male can inseminate several females.

Race Against Time

A single female lays an average of about 300 eggs, with larger females laying more than smaller ones. Egg-laying begins within a few days of mating, the female attaching the eggs singly to submerged vegetation. The eggs hatch after between two and five weeks, depending on water temperature. The larvae have bushy external gills and grow rapidly, feeding on a variety of invertebrate prey and on the tadpoles of frogs. Larval growth and development must be completed before the pond dries out, and the larvae seem to be able to speed up development when there is less rain to keep the pond filled.

Battling the Odds

The Santa Cruz long-toed salamander is protected by both California state and United States federal legislation. However, its habitat—small, marshy areas in Monterey Bay—is now surrounded by intensive agriculture, and there are only a handful of ponds left that are suitable for breeding. While habitat loss is the greatest threat, the Santa Cruz long-toed salamander is also threatened by drought which, if prolonged over years, could wipe out the remaining individuals.

Eggs from northern parts of the species' range have recently been found to be susceptible to the harmful effects of UV-B radiation. This suggests that the salamander may also be threatened by increased ultraviolet radiation; it is increasing because the ozone layer—a band of enriched oxygen found in the atmosphere that filters out harmful ultraviolet radiation—is being depleted as a result of pollution.

The Santa Cruz long-toed salamander *has a striking appearance; it is glossy black on the back and sides, with yellow or orange stripes or blotches and numerous white speckles on its flanks.*

Salmon, Danube

Hucho hucho

Unlike its oceangoing cousins, the Danube salmon lives, breeds, and dies in the inland waters of the Danube River, where it is exposed to habitat destruction and environmental pollution.

Salmon are majestic fish, and the Danube species is the largest of all. While the Danube salmon lives in rivers, many species live at sea. On reaching maturity, sea-dwelling salmon undertake a migration of epic proportions to the river in which they were spawned. Compelled by instinct, each fish battles against unbelievable odds—sometimes including rapids or even falls—to reach the mouth of its home river to spawn. The female digs pits in the gravel in which to lay her eggs, which take about five weeks to hatch.

Although the life cycle of sea-dwelling salmon is physically challenging, its migratory habits have helped safeguard its success as a species. Juveniles that manage to negotiate the journey from their spawning grounds to the sea stand a better chance of reaching maturity than those that stay in the rivers of their birth. Unlike the Danube salmon, sea salmon avoid exposure to the pollution or irreversible habitat alteration that can occur in rivers as a result of environmental disasters.

International Pressures

The Danube River flows through 12 countries inhabited by a total of more than 70 million people. Enforcement of environmental controls is therefore complicated. Some problems are historical, relating to industrial sites that were built before environmental

DATA PANEL

Danube salmon (European salmon, Danube trout, European river trout)

Hucho hucho

Family: Salmonidae

World population: Unknown; estimates are low

Distribution: Rivers of Danube basin; introduced elsewhere in Europe, U.S., Canada, and Morocco

Habitat: Deep, well-oxygenated regions of fast-flowing water; also found in backwaters at temperatures of 43–64°F (6–18°C)

Size: Up to 6.5 ft (2 m). Weight: over 220 lb (100 kg)

Form: Similar to salmon (*Salmo salar*), but slimmer; large head and jaws. Greenish back, silvery sides with diffused pink sheen, white along belly. Numerous small star-shaped black spots on back, gradually decreasing in number down body

Diet: Adults feed on other fish, amphibians, reptiles, waterfowl, and even small mammals. Juveniles feed predominantly on invertebrates

Breeding: Spawning March–May after migration to shallow, gravelly areas with fast-flowing, oxygen-rich water. Female excavates nest with tail and (with help of male) covers fertilized eggs. Hatching period 5 weeks

Related endangered species: Satsukimasa salmon (*Oncorhynchus ishikawai*) EN; carpione del Garda (*Salmo carpio*) VU; Ohrid trout (*S. letnica*) VU; ala Balik (*S. platycephalus*) CR; Adriatic salmon (*Salmothymus obtusirostris*) EN; beloribitsa (*Stenodus leucichthys leucichthys*) EN

Status: IUCN EN; not listed by CITES

See also: Drainage and Irrigation **1:** 40; Pollution **1:** 50; Galaxias, Swan **5:** 16

The Danube salmon *(also known as the European salmon, Danube trout, and European river trout) is the largest of all the salmons, and faces an uncertain future.*

legislation had to be taken into account. Others are political, where one country is not bound by the environmental laws of another. Both situations apply to the Danube, along which there are approximately 1,700 industries, many producing wastes that are known to be toxic. Aquatic organisms cannot survive the levels of toxicity and must find new areas or perish. Escape is not always possible, and the result is often the destruction of many thousands of creatures and their habitats.

Pollution Crises

In 2000 a dam leaked cyanide from a Romanian gold mine into the Tiza River, a tributary of the Danube, killing all forms of aquatic life for 250 miles (400 km) downstream. In Hungary alone about 85 tons of dead fish were removed. Some environmentalists claimed that the whole ecological system of the river had been wiped out by the spillage.

By early February 2000 cyanide was detected at the confluence of the Tiza with the Danube, and it was feared that the poisoning might cause the extinction of the Danube salmon. The outcome has been less devastating, but the situation illustrates the precarious future faced by the Danube salmon.

Such pollution crises are serious enough to threaten the existence of any Danube species. In the case of the Danube salmon there are other significant threats, including overfishing, water extraction for a wide range of industrial and other uses, and river alteration (primarily channeling and damming).

The Danube salmon is being pressurized from many quarters, to the extent that its long-term survival looks uncertain. Repeated attempts to introduce hatchery-bred stocks into a number of watercourses have been largely unsuccessful. However, in 1968 stocks were introduced from Czechoslovakia into Spanish waters, well outside the species' natural range. Over the years the stocks have become established. Restocking might not be the answer to the Danube salmon's problems, but it could be an essential lifeline.

Sandpiper, Spoon-Billed

Eurynorhynchus pygmeus

Its small population and precise nesting requirements, and especially habitat disturbance at its migration and wintering sites, have made the future of the spoon-billed sandpiper uncertain.

The spoon-billed sandpiper has an extraordinary bill with an expanded diamond-shaped "spoon" tip. The bill is an adaptation to the bird's unusual feeding technique, in which it moves through shallow water, rapidly turning its head from side to side so that its bill sweeps the water's surface in semicircles. As with other sandpipers, the bill has touch-sensitive cells at its tip that can detect the movements of tiny invertebrates living in water or soft mud. The widened tip probably gives the bird a larger area of sensitivity to the vibrations caused by its prey and allows it to take in more with each snap.

Unlike many waders, which nest in a variety of coastal habitats, spoon-billed sandpipers have exacting requirements. They visit their breeding haunts in summer, a narrow band of coast around the Chukotski Peninsula in northeastern Siberia, and, farther south, along the isthmus (narrow strip of land) connecting the peninsula with the island of Kamchatka. Within their restricted breeding range they choose only sandy ridges with sparse vegetation along the shores of shallow coastal lagoons. They also prefer the inner parts of bays where certain river estuaries enter the sea, forming a complex patchwork of water channels and moss-covered shingle banks. Such specific requirements account for their patchy distribution within their overall range.

Winter Quarters

Every fall the spoon-billed sandpiper undergoes a long and potentially hazardous journey to the coasts of subtropical

DATA PANEL

Spoon-billed sandpiper

Eurynorhynchus pygmeus

Family: Scolopacidae

World population: 4,000–6,000 birds (estimated); possibly even fewer than 1,000 breeding pairs

Distribution: Breeds in northeastern Siberia, Russia; winters in South and Southeast Asia

Habitat: Nests on coasts with sandy ridges near marshes and lakes; winters on coasts, especially by deltas and lagoons

Size: Length: 5.5–6.3 in (14–16 cm). Weight: male about 1 oz (29.5 g); female about 1.3 oz (35 g)

Form: Small, plump-bodied bird with distinctive spatula-shaped bill. In breeding plumage has dark-streaked, reddish-brown head, neck, and breast; blackish back; buff and pale-reddish fringes to wing feathers; white belly; black legs and bill. In nonbreeding plumage has pale-grayish upperparts, prominent white stripe above eyes, and all-white underparts. Juveniles similar to winter adults, but browner

Diet: Insects and their larvae, both land-dwelling and aquatic, including beetles, flies, and small wasps; other aquatic invertebrates such as crustaceans; also small seeds

Breeding: In June and July scrapes out a hollow, sometimes lined with leaves, among low vegetation; 4 brown-blotched buff eggs are laid; incubation 18–20 days; fledging period 15–20 days. Male matures at 2 years, female probably at 1 year

Related endangered species: Nine other species of sandpipers and relatives, including the eskimo curlew (*Numenius borealis*)* CR; slender-billed curlew (*N. tenuirostris*) CR; spotted greenshank (*Tringa guttifer*) EN, and Tuamotu sandpiper (*Prosobonia cancellata*) EN

Status: IUCN VU; not listed by CITES

See also: Specialization **1:** 28; Murrelet, Japanese **7:** 4; Stilt, Black **9:** 32

and tropical South and Southeast Asia for the winter. The females leave first; their mates tend their brood of chicks when they are between five and six days old for a further 10 to15 days. The males then leave, and eventually, so do the young; some young linger on in the nesting grounds until mid-October. In their winter quarters the sandpipers prefer deltas and lagoons with mud banks, sand banks, or islets (small islands).

Precisely where the spoon-billed sandpipers go and what conditions they require in winter is still largely a mystery. Birdwatchers have recorded the spoon-billed sandpipers from eastern India and Sri Lanka to Thailand, Vietnam, the Malaysian Peninsula, Singapore, the Philippines, and China. Because numbers are so small, it has been difficult to build up a clear picture of the bird's wintering range and to distinguish it from places where the birds are simply rare wanderers. In 1989, however, 257 individuals were counted on islands off the delta of the Ganges River in the Bay of Bengal, indicating a major site. Other wintering sites discovered since then with more than 10 birds include one with 50 birds in southeastern Bangladesh and another in Orissa, east-central India, with 48

birds. However, in 1993 only three birds were recorded during the whole of the Asian Waterfowl Census.

Uncertain Future

Always rare, the species now appears to be in serious trouble. Recent surveys showed that numbers were far lower than expected at known sites, indicating that the bird is undergoing a dramatic decline. There are no obvious reasons for this within the sandpiper's breeding range, where habitat degradation and human disturbance currently have only local effects.

Conservationists think that the major threats to the species are to its migration flyway and wintering sites. Tidal flats are being reclaimed for industry, infrastructure, and aquaculture, and becoming increasingly polluted. The important stopover site for the migrants at Saemankuem, South Korea, has been partially reclaimed, and the remaining wetlands are under serious threat. Further research and conservation action are urgently required before this unusual Arctic wader reaches the brink of extinction.

The spoon-billed sandpiper *has a bill with a broad and flattened tip.*

Scrub-Bird, Noisy

Atrichornis clamosus

Rediscovered in 1961, the rarely seen noisy scrub-bird is a splendid advertisement for what can be done by a concerted and informed conservation effort over a period of 35 years. However, it still has a very small total population.

The scrub-birds belong to an ancient family of songbirds found only in Australia. Apart from the noisy scrub-bird there is only one other species, the also rare but less threatened rufous scrub-bird found in the mountain forests of eastern Australia. The songbirds may have evolved about 50 million years ago in the Eocene epoch, when much of southern Australia was covered by rain forest of southern beech trees or shrubs.

In Western Australia climatic changes led to the disappearance of forest cover. The noisy scrub-bird was able to survive only in isolated populations in moist forest areas in the southwest of its former range. Although now a relict species, it managed to hang on in its restricted habitat.

However, things changed dramatically when European settlers arrived in the area in the 19th century. Prior to this, traditional land management by the Aboriginal population included regular, small-scale burning of shrublands, resulting in a mosaic of dense cover and open areas that suited the scrub-bird.

Within 50 years of the settlers' arrival, however, the wildlife-friendly practices had been almost entirely replaced by a regime involving frequent, large-scale burning every two years to provide grazing for livestock. Together with the greatly increased incidence of "accidental wildfires" and drainage and clearance of swampy scrubland for agriculture, this had a devastating effect on the numbers and range of the noisy scrub-bird. It also had an impact on other, now equally rare species of the region.

Rediscovery

The noisy scrub-bird was first recorded by Western science in 1842 at Drakesbrook, 62 miles (100 km) south of Perth, on the west coast of the state of Western Australia. Until 1889 it was also identified at five other coastal sites between Perth and Albany on the south coast of Western Australia. From 1889, however, no more birds were found, despite many searches during the early decades of the 20th century. By the 1950s many ornithologists thought that it must be extinct. Then, in

---

DATA PANEL

Noisy scrub-bird

Atrichornis clamosus

Family: Atrichornithidae

World population: About 1,500 birds

Distribution: Restricted to small area on south coast of Western Australia

Habitat: Shrubland with both dense clumps of low-growing eucalypts, banksias, and other shrubs, sedges, or accumulated plant debris for nesting; small, open areas with a dense layer of leaf-litter for feeding. All occupied sites have not been burned for over 10 years

Size: Length: 8.8–10.3 in (22–26 cm)

Form: Thrush-sized bird with triangular profile to head; large, dark eyes, short, rounded wings, long, rounded tail, and powerful legs; upperparts dark brown with fine black bars, red-brown wings; underparts merging gray-brown to cream on lower breast and red-brown on vent and undertail; male has black triangular patch on throat bordered by white stripes; female has white throat. Juvenile has unbarred upperparts and buff foreneck and breast

Diet: Mainly ground-dwelling insects, and occasionally seeds; small frogs and lizards fed to nestlings

Breeding: Usually June–October. Domed nest of grasses, rushes, or dead leaves with side entrance made in clumps of rushes or dense shrubs about 8 in (20 cm) above ground. Single pale-buff egg with orange-brown blotches is incubated for 5–5.5 weeks; young fledge in 3–4 weeks

Related endangered species: Rufous scrub-bird (*Atrichornis rufescens*) LRnt

Status: IUCN VU; CITES I

AUSTRALIA

Western Australia

See also: Natural Disasters 1: 57; Reintroduction 1: 92; Finch, Gouldian 4: 74

1961 the noisy scrub-bird was rediscovered at Two Peoples Bay, near Albany. It had managed to survive there because the terrain—rocky, hilly headland backed by sand dunes and lakes—was unsuitable for agriculture.

Noisy scrub-birds are extremely elusive. They use their limited powers of flight to move from shrub to shrub, and the camouflage of their subtly patterned plumage hides them from view. However, the loud territorial song of the male can be heard throughout the breeding season and also at other times of the year. It is a distinctive series of notes in a descending scale, accelerating into an ear-splitting finale.

Success Story

At the time of its rediscovery in 1961 the noisy scrub-bird was restricted almost entirely to the Mount Gardner area of Two Peoples Bay. There followed an intense debate between conservationists and developers; luckily, the conservationists won the day. In 1967 the Two Peoples Bay Nature Reserve was established, chiefly to protect the noisy scrub-bird and two other local rarities, the similar-looking western bristlebird and the western whipbird.

An intensive program of conservation began in 1976. It included the translocation of birds from the Mount Gardner population to other suitable sites, as well as vigilance to prevent damage from fires. The

The noisy scrub-bird *spends much of its time in dense cover. It scurries around on or close to the ground or burrows into deep leaf litter to look for insects.*

program has resulted in an increase in the species' range and numbers: Today there are at least five populations in the region around Two Peoples Bay that are gradually uniting. An introduced population at nearby Bald Island and a reintroduced population at Drakesbrook, where the species was first identified by Western science, are both doing well.

Wildfires and the inappropriate management of planned fires remain a serious potential threat to the species. In 1994 a fire wiped out most of a recently translocated population at Mount Taylor, and the few remaining birds disappeared within a year. By contrast, unusually heavy winter rainfall caused declines at Gardner Lake in 1988 and 1991. Habitat destruction on private land might affect dispersal and fragment populations. However, it is hoped that continued vigilance by conservationists will be able to prevent any further reductions in population.

Sea Anemone, Starlet

Nematostella vectensis

The starlet sea anemone was not discovered until 1929. Its small size and burrowing lifestyle make the animal difficult to study. The same factors also make an assessment of the threats to its survival problematic.

The starlet anemone was first discovered in the mud at the bottom of a rock pool at Bembridge on the Isle of Wight in the English Channel in 1929. The first scientific description of it did not appear until 1935.

The starlet is one of the least known and smallest of the 1,000 or more species of sea anemone. It measures just 0.3 to 0.7 inches (1 to 2 cm) long. It is difficult to make out much of its structural detail without the aid of a low-powered microscope.

Most small, aquatic creatures are very sensitive to the amount of salt present in water—the salinity. However, a feature of the starlet sea anemone is its ability to tolerate a wide range of salinities, from about 9 parts salt per thousand parts water to 37.7 parts salt per thousand parts water. (Normal coastal seawater is about 34 parts salt per thousand parts water.) The starlet anemone therefore thrives in environments such as lagoons and salt marshes in which salinity fluctuates. It favors coastal lagoons where fine mud overlies gravel or shingle. It has also been found in brackish creeks and pools in salt marshes.

Unlike many sea anemones, the starlet lacks a structure called an adhesive basal disk, which allows it to attach itself to rocks and shell. Instead, it has a burrowing organ called a physa that enables it to burrow into mud from where it can remain hidden and protected in wait for its prey. The physa does, however, have small adherent spots, called rugae, that stick to surfaces such as pebbles and pieces of vegetation so that the animal can exist without sediment in to which to burrow. Because they become attached to pieces of algae or seaweed, starlet sea anemones are collected inadvertently.

Patient Predator

Like all sea anemones, the starlet is an opportunistic, sit-and-wait predator. Its oral disk (mouth) is surrounded by two rings of transparent tentacles: an outer ring of six long, trailing tentacles and an inner ring of seven shorter, upstanding ones. The tentacles

DATA PANEL

Starlet sea anemone
(Isle of Wight anemone)

Nematostella vectensis

Family: Edwardsiidae

World population: Unknown

Distribution: Coastal lagoons in northwestern Europe and the U.S.

Habitat: Brackish (slightly salty) lagoons; ponds in salt marshes

Size: Length: 0.3–0.7 in (1–2 cm)

Form: Cylindrical, transparent body; twin circles of tentacles surrounding mouth; hollow tentacles. The transparent, jellylike substance that makes up most of body, as in a jellyfish, is called mesogloea

Diet: Animal plankton (minute, drifting animals)

Breeding: Unknown

Related endangered species: Ivell's sea anemone *(Edwardsia ivelli)* Data Deficient

Status: IUCN VU; not listed by CITES

See also: Pollution 1: 50; Research 1: 84; Cushion Star 3: 88; Sea Fan, Broad 8: 60

are armed with stinging cells that can immobilize and subdue animal plankton (tiny animals that drift at the water's surface) that collide with them.

Threats to Survival

Small, burrowing species such as the starlet sea anemone are difficult to find and even more difficult to study and assess in terms of their vulnerability and conservation status. There are probably many thousands of small, short-lived invertebrates, as yet undiscovered, whose precise status would be equally difficult to establish. A relative of the starlet anemone, for example, Ivell's sea anemone, was discovered in a brackish lagoon in Sussex on the south coast of England. The two species are very similar in appearance, but the distribution of Ivell's sea anemone appears to be extremely limited. Recent attempts to relocate the animal have failed, raising the question of whether Ivell's sea anemone has become extinct.

The starlet sea anemone *is less than an inch long. Like other sea anemones, it has a hollow, cylindrical body (polyp) with a ring of tentacles around the mouth.*

The main threat to the starlet sea anemone is urban development and human activities along the coast. Its brackish lagoon habitat is under pressure both from developers and from changes to drainage and sediment accumulation caused by human populations. The dumping of rubbish in the vicinity of lagoons is also a threat, since it can result in an increase in nitrogen levels in the water. This can cause a rapid growth surge in aquatic algae—an algal bloom. Algal blooms cause adverse physical and chemical changes in the water; they can result in the depletion of nutrients available to other species and release poisons into the environment. Such factors could be a threat not only to the starlet sea anemone but also to other as yet undiscovered species.

Sea Fan, Broad

Eunicella verrucosa

The sea fan is a type of coral made up of many simple polyps joined together to form a colony in a fanlike pattern. In common with a number of other marine invertebrates, sea fans are beautiful and often form major attractions in "submarine gardens." A slow-growing animal, it is now under threat from overcollection.

Sea fans are found in most of the world's seas and oceans. They may grow from shallow water down to the edge of the continental shelves and beyond; they are even found at depths of about 13,000 feet (4,000 m) in some parts of the world. The broad sea fan occurs in the northeastern Atlantic and in the Mediterranean Sea. Sea fans are attractive to souvenir hunters, and thoughtless collecting by divers has recently reduced their populations around European coasts.

Sea fans are colonial, that is, they are made up of many individual polyps, or zooids—cylindrical forms joined together to form a colony. Such a lifestyle is not unusual in the phylum Cnidaria to which they belong. In the broad sea fan the polyps are arranged in two rows along the top and bottom of the branches.

Each polyp is a miniature animal in its own right and has its own mouth that also serves as its anus. The mouth is surrounded by eight minute branching tentacles that are armed with stinging cells. The tentacle form is a feature of the order Gorgonacea (horny corals) and is ideal for sieving the passing water currents to trap microscopic plankton. Once collected, the prey is manipulated into the gastric cavity via the mouth. The gastric cavity extends into a number of tubes that increase the surface area for absorption and digestion of food products. Many species of sea fan are virtually two dimensional, and they grow so that the colony faces the prevailing currents at right angles, thus maximizing their ability to catch prey. Growth is slow, so some sea fans are very old.

The colony is supported by an internal horny skeleton made up of a substance called gorgonin. The tissue from which the polyps are made is further supported and protected by crystals of calcium carbonate that are embedded within it.

DATA PANEL

Broad sea fan

Eunicella verrucosa

Family: Anthozoa

World population: Unknown

Distribution: Mediterranean Sea; northeastern Atlantic; off coasts of France, Ireland, U.K., Mauritania, Morocco, Portugal, and Spain

Habitat: Rocks and hard surfaces from 49 ft (15 m) downward to about 984 ft (300 m)

Size: Colony grows to 11.8 in (30 cm) in height

Form: Plantlike pink or white colony made up of polyps—cylindrical sessile (attached) forms; branches in 1 plane only. Individual polyps arranged in double rows

Diet: Minute drifting plankton

Breeding: Details not well known; planula (free-swimming larva) results from fertilization of eggs; attaches itself to a new substrate; develops into a new colony, which produces new zooids

Related endangered species: Probably many, including red coral (*Corallium rubrum*)

Status: IUCN VU; not listed by CITES

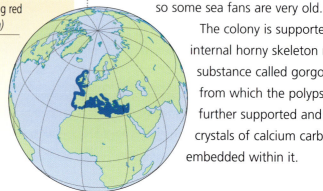

See also: Luxury Products **1:** 46; Cushion Star **3:** 88; Sea Anemone, Starlet **8:** 58

Sperms and eggs develop inside the polyps, and fertilization results in the development of a planula (free-swimming larva), which escapes from the "parent" via its mouth and swims into the sea. The planula has a simple structure and is covered with microscopic beating filaments (cilia) that drive it through the water. However, the planula can detect a suitable substratum—usually rock—on which to settle and develop into a new colony, producing at first a founder polyp. The polyp grows and produces more individual polyps and the necessary skeleton so that a colony structure is developed once again.

Vulnerability

The emerging interest in marine conservation has led to an increased awareness of the effects of overcollection and human disturbance on some marine animals and plants. Although it has not been significantly at risk in the past, threats to the broad

Sea fans *come in a variety of colors, from deep red, yellow, and orange to pink and white. The polyps spread out their tentacles, forming a net with which they catch plankton.*

sea fan have risen recently with the increase in popularity of scuba diving. The broad sea fan and its Mediterranean relative, red coral (*Corallium rubrum*), are both slow growing, so they are potentially more vulnerable. Unlike the broad sea fan, *Corallium* has been collected for centuries, certainly since classical times. A rich red color, it was considered semiprecious and made into jewelry by the Greeks and Romans; it was also thought to be able to ward off illnesses. *Corallium* is now scarce in the Mediterranean and is found only at great depths. Collection of the animal seems as yet to be poorly regulated.

Sea Lion, Steller's

Eumetopias jubatus

Steller's sea lion was once considered a pest because of the quantities of fish it "stole" from humans. Now the situation has been reversed; Steller's sea lions are in decline because we eat too much of their food.

Although it is a widespread species, the number of Steller's sea lions has been declining since the 1980s, when there were about 290,000; today there are fewer than 89,000. The western population, which extends across the Aleutian Islands to Japan, appears to be shrinking relatively slowly. The main losses seem to have occurred in the eastern population along the coasts of California, Oregon, British Columbia, and southern Alaska. Although the population there may still number about 39,000, it has declined by 83 percent in 30 years. If an animal population decreases that fast, action must be taken before it is too late.

Steller's sea lion used to be hunted for its meat, hide, and blubber, but commercial hunting stopped in the 1970s. About 400 are still killed each year for traditional uses by the indigenous peoples of Alaska (the skins make good canoe covers). Marine mammals in American waters have full legal protection, so large-scale killing of Steller's sea lions or disturbance of their breeding places should be prevented now and is unlikely to be the main cause of their decline. However, the animals are sometimes caught up in fishing nets. Around Vancouver Island licenses were issued to kill a few sea lions that were causing problems in fish-farming areas, and some illegal killing still goes on.

Oil spills and contamination of food by chemicals pose another threat to Steller's sea lion, as they do to many other species. Around Japan high levels of tributyl tin (TBT) have been reported in the bodies of sea lions. This is a poisonous substance found in the paint used to prevent barnacles from attaching to the hulls of boats.

Despite such hazards, the basic problem for Steller's sea lion seems to be a reduction in its food supply. The animals feed on fish,

DATA PANEL

Steller's sea lion (northern sea lion)

Eumetopias jubatus

Family: Otariidae

World population: Fewer than 89,000

Distribution: Edges of North Pacific and Bering Sea

Habitat: Coastal waters, offshore rocks and islands; also sea caves

Size: Length: male 9.2–10.5 ft (2.8–3.2 m); female 7.5–9.5 ft (2.3–2.9 m). Weight: male 1,240–2,470 lb (566–1,120 kg); female 580–770 lb (263–350 kg)

Form: Seal with coat of short, coarse hair; small ears; longer flippers than true seals. Males have manes

Diet: Fish, particularly pollock, salmon, herring, mackerel; sometimes squid and octopus

Breeding: Single pup born per year after 12-month gestation. Mature at about 4 years. Life span over 30 years in females, lower in males

Related endangered species: Guadeloupe fur seal (*Arctocephalus townsendii*) VU; Galápagos fur seal (*A. galapagoensis*) VU; Juan Fernandez fur seal (*A. philippii*) VU; northern fur seal (*Callorhinus ursinus*)* VU; Hooker's sea lion (*Phocarctos hookeri*) VU

Status: IUCN EN; not listed by CITES

See also: Hunting **1:** 42; Pollution **1:** 50; Seal, Northen Fur **8:** 78

which they catch on or near the seabed, sometimes diving down to more than 1,200 feet (400 m) to get them. Trawlers harvest the same fish by dragging huge nets across the seabed. This competition for fish is a problem for the sea lions, especially around sea lion breeding colonies, where mother sea lions feed for up to three days at a time before returning to suckle their pups on the beaches.

Action against Fishing

Intensive commercial fishing has left fish stocks—especially walleye pollock—severely depleted. Trawlers were banned from fishing near sea lion breeding places throughout the 1990s. Exclusion zones were then extended to keep trawlers at least 22 miles (35 km) away from the colonies, and fishing restrictions were imposed all year round, not just in the breeding season. Fishermen were also made to spread their activities to reduce the pressure on fish stocks in certain areas. Around the Aleutian Islands, for instance, restrictions were placed

Steller's sea lion is in decline as a result of overfishing, but other factors may be at work too, including changes in sea currents.

on fishing for mackerel (another important food for the sea lions), and trawling for pollock was forbidden.

Such measures have come about partly as a result of lobbying by environmental campaigners. They must be taken seriously in order for us to prevent unpredictable and possibly irreversible damage to the North Pacific ecosystem and the extinction of Steller's sea lion.

Sea-Eagle, Steller's

Haliaeetus pelagicus

One of the world's largest and most impressive birds of prey, Steller's sea-eagle breeds only in the far east of Russia. There, and in its major wintering sites in Japan, its declining population faces a variety of continuing threats.

Not only is Steller's sea-eagle one of the biggest of the world's birds of prey, but it is one of the most recognizable due to its striking plumage. When hunting, the rare predator concentrates mainly on fish, especially Pacific salmon. As well as killing live fish, it will also scavenge for dead and dying salmon that become stranded during their spawning runs upriver. During periods when its staple diet is in short supply, Steller's sea-eagle will switch to hunting mammals and birds. Sometimes the eagles are reduced to searching out smaller prey such as crabs and mollusks. Also, the great birds eat considerable amounts of carrion in winter.

Adaptable Hunter

A Steller's sea-eagle usually locates much of its food without taking to the air, using a technique known as "still hunting" that is practiced by many other raptors (from the Latin word "raptor," meaning a plunderer). Perched on a suitable lookout, it patiently scans the area. As soon as it spots prey, it swoops down to seize it in its talons. When hunting spawning salmon in shallow water, the eagle often simply wades in and uses the long, sharp hook of its massive beak like a fisherman's gaff (a hook-tipped pole). Pairs of eagles that nest near seabird colonies use another technique; patroling the tall sea cliffs, they suddenly veer close to the nesting ledges and panic the auks or gulls. As the terrified adults take wing, the eagles snatch them in midair or pluck a defenseless chick from the ledge.

Declining Population

As well as a good food supply, the eagles need secure breeding sites. Most pairs breed in the tops of tall trees; if none are available, the eagles will also nest on cliffs. After performing aerobatic courtship displays to strengthen their bond, a pair will repair their great stick

DATA PANEL

Steller's sea-eagle

Haliaeetus pelagicus

Family: Accipitridae

World population: Estimated at 5,000 birds

Distribution: Breeds only on Kamchatka Peninsula, coasts around Sea of Okhotsk, lower reaches of River Amur, and Sakhalin and Shantar islands. Some birds winter in Kamchatka and around Sea of Okhotsk, but most do so in southern Kuril Islands (Russia) and Hokkaido Island (Japan)

Habitat: Breeds on coasts and inland near lakes or rivers. Nests in mature trees or cliffs. Birds wintering in Russia stay mainly on coasts; those wintering in Japan stay near coasts or fresh water; some move to mountains

Size: Length: 33.5–37 in (85–94 cm); wingspan: 7.2–8 ft (2.2–2.5 m); female larger than male. Weight: 11–20 lb (4.9–9 kg)

Form: Huge eagle with massive, powerfully hooked orange-yellow bill; distinctive plumage: blackish-brown except for white shoulders, forehead, thighs, rump, and wedge-shaped tail; legs and feet orange-yellow

Diet: Living or dead fish, especially salmon; birds up to the size of geese; mammals, including hares, Arctic foxes, and young seals

Breeding: Huge nest of sticks, usually built high up in tree, sometimes on a cliff; female lays 2 white eggs, typically between mid-April and early May; incubation takes about 5.5–6.5 weeks; usually only 1 young survives; fledges in about 10 weeks

Related endangered species: Gray-headed fish-eagle (*Ichthyophaga ichthyaetus*) LRnt; lesser fish-eagle (*I. humilis*) LRnt; Madagascar fish-eagle (*Haliaeetus vociferoides*) CR; Pallas's sea-eagle (*H. leucoryphus*) VU; Sanford's fish-eagle (*H. sanfordi*) VU; white-tailed eagle (*H. albicilla*) LRnt

Status: IUCN VU; CITES I and II

See also: A Tale of Two Eagles **1:** 94; Vulture, Cape Griffon **10:** 34

steller's sea-eagle faces threats from the timber industry: Much of the old forest that provides the eagle with tall, mature trees for nesting has been logged for timber.

Moreover, high levels of the pesticides DDT and DDE are to be found in the environment. Industrial pollutants known as PCBs are also present in the Khabarovsk Territory on the eastern shore of the Sea of Okhotsk and around Magadan on its northern coast.

On Hokkaido Island, Japan, where the major proportion of the population winters, overfishing has caused serious declines in fish stocks—as it has in

Steller's sea-eagle *has a distinctive beak that is massive, strongly arched, and bright orange-yellow like its legs and feet. An efficient and adaptable hunter, the eagle sometimes uses its beak to pluck fish from shallow water.*

nests, which they generally use year after year. An old nest may be as much as 12 feet (3.6 m) deep and 8 feet (2.4 m) wide. The female's normal clutch is two eggs, but most pairs raise only a single eaglet every other year. Chick mortality from falling out of the nest, nest collapse, or disease, can therefore be significant.

Sadly, the Steller's sea-eagle has suffered increasingly from disturbance to its habitat. The remote areas where it lives have become subject to heavy development. Major threats include hydroelectric power projects and proposed coastal and offshore petrochemical exploitation, which will affect the bird's food supply. In its Russian breeding grounds

the eagle's breeding range. The lack of fish has led to increasing numbers of eagles wintering inland, where many scavenge on carcasses of sika deer abandoned by hunters. While feeding, the birds are in danger of swallowing the lead shot that killed the deer. Researchers predict that lead poisoning will cause the already vulnerable population to halve in just 50 years.

Conservation Measures

Conservationists have set up feeding stations to deter the eagles from consuming contaminated deer. Other targets include regular testing of the birds and their environment for lead, pesticides, and industrial pollutants. Mitigating the effects of coastal development on the Russian breeding grounds is another aim, along with the protection of salmon spawning rivers. Efforts are also being made to manage fish stocks in a sustainable way.

Sea-Urchin, Edible

Echinus esculentus

Sadly, the beautifully colored edible sea-urchin has become a familiar sight in beach souvenir shops. The animal is collected extensively because its test (shell-like internal skeleton) makes popular decorative objects and souvenirs.

Sea-urchins are spiny-skinned invertebrates that are in the same phylum—Echinodermata—as sea lilies, starfish, brittle stars, and sea cucumbers. Like other echinoderms, they have no head and no true brain, and their bodies have a skeleton of chalky plates. There are about 800 species of sea-urchin.

Sea-urchins are important grazers in marine communities. By eating young and developing algae (plants without true stems, roots, and leaves), they play a major role in controlling vegetation growth in the sea. They also feed on encrusting animals such as barnacles and sea mats. A lack of sea-urchins in a given area can result in rapid algal growth, and in some sensitive habitats such as coral reefs this can have serious effects on other organisms; the plants quickly outcompete the slower-growing corals for light and space.

The edible sea-urchin is a temperate species, living on hard substrates and among larger algae in coastal waters around northwestern Europe. Compared with other species of sea-urchin, it is quite large and has a pale, rosy-pink test. The test is the shell-like internal skeleton that is so close to the outside of the animal that it appears to be a shell. However, it is covered by thin living tissue. The skeleton of sea-urchins, as in other echinoderms, is made up of crystals of calcium carbonate perforated by spaces. (As a result, it is easily occupied by minerals after the animal's death, so it fossilizes well.)

The sea-urchin's test bears whitish-pink needle-shaped spines with purple tips. They are used for defense against predators and as an aid to the animal's movement. Between the spines are the pedicellariae—minute pincerlike organs carried on stalks—that are used for grooming.

As well as spines sea-urchins also have many long, branched tentacles, called tube-feet, with suckers on the end, which are arranged in rows up and down the animals. They are hollow and can be filled with water from inside the animal and extended by hydraulic pressure. They are used for movement and balance, and in some species help act as a sort of camouflage.

Like other sea-urchins, the edible sea-urchin has a mouth on the underside of the test with a complex arrangement of five jaws with teeth that are extruded (thrust out) to scrape

DATA PANEL

Edible sea-urchin

Echinus esculentus

Family: Echinidae

World population: Unknown

Distribution: Northeastern Atlantic

Habitat: Rocks and seaweeds from the low tide mark down to 164 ft (50 m)

Size: Up to 6.7 in (17 cm) diameter; often smaller

Form: Globular body with calcareous test bearing movable spines and extendible tube-feet ending in suckers

Diet: Encrusting animals such as barnacles; large algae

Breeding: Seasonal spawning; fertilization occurs in the open water; free-swimming larva feeds on minute drifting plants until it metamorphoses to form a juvenile urchin

Related endangered species: Probably several, including the rock borer *Paracentrotus lividus* (no common name) not listed by IUCN. The species has been seriously overfished for its edible roe in parts of France and Ireland

Status: IUCN LRnt; not listed by CITES

See also: The Animal Kingdom **1:** 58; Cushion Star **3:** 88

algae and other encrusting plant and animal life from the rocks. When removed from the test but still joined together, the jaws resemble a Greek lantern; Aristotle referred to them as lantern teeth, and today the jaw arrangement is called an Aristotle's lantern.

Hunted Out

The edible sea-urchin was for centuries fished for its roe (eggs); the food was considered a delicacy in Tudor times (between 1485 and 1603). Unlike the smaller Mediterranean species *Paracentrotus lividus*, which has a more delicate roe, the relatively coarse roe of the edible sea-urchin is no longer considered desirable to eat.

The edible sea-urchin, *which used to be fished for its edible roe (eggs), is now collected for its beautiful test.*

The species is easily seen and collected under water. When the test is cleaned out by removing the intestine and reproductive organs, it makes an attractive ornament. In recent decades divers have collected edible sea-urchins from southwestern Britain in such large numbers that scientists now believe that a population crash may be imminent. However, further information is needed about the state of the natural populations of edible sea-urchin around northwestern Europe and the sea-urchin's life span so that measures can be taken to protect them.

Seahorse, Knysna

Hippocampus capensis

With their miniature bony-plated bodies, curled tails, and horselike heads, seahorses are distinctive in their appearance and remarkable in many other ways. Seahorses are harvested for the souvenir trade, but the Knysna seahorse is also threatened by the effects of tourism on its native habitat.

Seahorses are unusual fish, partly because of their armor-plated bodies and their upright swimming position. They lack the caudal (tail) fin that we normally associate with fish. Instead, there is a true tail that can be curled up and extended almost like the prehensile (adapted for grasping) tail of a monkey or a chameleon. Seahorses use their tails to cling onto vegetation and other objects, or even each other. Camouflage is another property that seahorses have that distinguishes them from many other fish. As well as being able to change color, seahorses can also develop elongations and other skin growths that allow them to blend in so effectively with their surroundings that they can become virtually invisible. This ability is best seen in seahorse species usually referred to as sea dragons (*Phycodorus eques* and *Phyllopteryx taeniolatus*), which are covered with outgrowths that look remarkably like seaweed. Another unusual characteristic of seahorses is that they are monogamous. Monogamy—the pairing up of a male and female for life or, as in the case of seahorses, for a breeding season or more—is not a trait that is normally encountered among fish.

Most amazing of all are the seahorse's breeding habits. In a total reversal of what we find in other animals, it is the male seahorse that incubates the eggs. Following an intricate courtship ritual, the pair face each other, and the female releases a batch of eggs into the male's abdominal brood pouch. Further batches are added to the original one until anything from 50 to 1,500 eggs (depending on the species) have been produced. They are later self-fertilized by the males. Parental duties become the exclusive responsibility of the male, which incubates the eggs. Once these eggs are ready to hatch, the male goes through a series of convulsions and contractions, gradually releasing the tiny juvenile seahorses, which are left to fend for themselves.

DATA PANEL

Knysna seahorse (Cape seahorse)

Hippocampus capensis

Family: Syngnathidae

World population: A few hundred

Distribution: Knysna Estuary, Cape Province, South Africa; also in a few bays in the surrounding region

Habitat: Submerged estuarine meadows ranging in depth from about 20 in–66 ft (50 cm–20 m)

Size: Length: 2–4.3 in (5–11 cm)

Form: Bony-plated body and horselike head with tubular snout (short in comparison to nearest relatives). Forward-curled tails. Coloration greenish or brownish, usually mottled; may also have dark body spots. Lacks the coronet (crownlike structure on top of the head) found in many other seahorse species

Diet: Small aquatic invertebrates

Breeding: Repeated matings and broods between September and April at water temperatures above 68°F (20°C). Female releases batches of eggs into male's abdominal pouch; eggs are self-fertilized by the male; male gives birth to 7–95 fry (young) after gestation period of 14–21 days. Maturity is reached in about 1 year

Related endangered species: Thirty-five species of seahorse, sea dragon, and pipe fish (all members of the family Syngnathidae) are listed as Vulnerable by the IUCN; 7 are listed as Data Deficient

Status: IUCN EN; not listed by CITES

Trade in Seahorses

No fewer than 46 countries and regions are involved in the seahorse trade, with annual exports from the main suppliers ranging from 3 to 15 tons. Even if these figures were to relate

See also: Life Strategies 1: 24; Eel, Lesser Spiny 4: 62

to live "fresh" or deep-frozen seahorses, the actual numbers of specimens involved would be colossal. When we consider that the data relate to dried specimens, which are only a fraction of the weight of live ones, the weights translate into many millions of individual seahorses.

Seahorses are thought by some Asian communities—particularly but not exclusively the Chinese—to be able to cure a host of illnesses and Traditional Chinese medicine undoubtedly accounts for much of the world demand for the animals.

The souvenir trade is also a large-scale consumer of seahorses. They are sold as dried and varnished specimens and made into a host of small decorative objects such as keyrings, paperweights, and so on.

Collections of live specimens for home aquaria also play a part in the seahorse trade. Even conservative estimates show that collecting could represent a significant additional pressure on wild populations of many species of seahorse.

In the case of the Knysna seahorse, which is found west of Port Elizabeth in Cape Province, South Africa, collection for the souvenir trade and aquaria does not appear to be the major cause of decline. Tourism and pollution, however, have put the species at risk. Tourism is responsible for creating pressure on the estuary around Knysna Lagoon, where freshwater floods have caused heavy mortalities among the resident seahorse population. Increasing levels of pollution mean that even captive-bred specimens cannot be released into their home waters.

The damaging effects of tourism, allied to the restricted range of the species and its extreme rarity, led to the Knysna seahorse being classified by the IUCN as Endangered in 1996.

Seahorses are weak swimmers. They cling to seaweed and propel themselves along with their fins, rising and falling by altering the amount of air in their swim bladders. The Knysna seahorse lacks the crownlike structure on the top of the head that is found in many other species.

Conservation

Research studies on wild populations are seen as a vital step in establishing the actual status of seahorse species around the world. A major industry-backed project, the Global Marine Aquarium Database, launched in 2000, should help identify the main species that are traded, assisting in the establishment of sustainable harvesting policies and identifying which species may be in need of protection.

Captive breeding of the Knysna seahorse has been undertaken using adult specimens supplied by the South African government. Attempts are also being made to control conditions in the natural habitat; if successful, the release of captive-bred specimens into their home waters may be possible.

Seal, Baikal

Phoca sibirica

The icy waters of Siberia's Lake Baikal are a challenging place to live at the best of times. The added problems of disease, pollution, and a long-established sealing industry are putting the Baikal seal under intolerable pressure.

Lake Baikal in Siberia is the deepest and oldest lake in the world. It is home to many remarkable plants and animals, including the only species of seal that spends its entire life in and around fresh water: the Baikal seal.

There is a long history of seal hunting on Lake Baikal, with pelts, meat, and oil providing an important contribution to the local economy. In the 1930s overhunting was seriously threatening the Baikal seals, and a system of quotas was introduced, allowing only limited numbers to be hunted each year. The population recovered steadily, and concern for the species subsided. However, in recent years the seals' fortunes appear to have taken a turn for the worse. Between 1994 and 2000 the population declined by as much as 20 percent. There are several interrelated reasons for this alarming development.

Victims of the Hunt

In the late 1990s seal-hunting quotas stood at about 6,000 seals per year. However, the figure did not include the many seals that were killed or injured in the hunt but not removed from the water. Some reports suggest that for every seal landed, a further three died but sank before they could be retrieved. Poaching

DATA PANEL

Baikal seal (nerpa)

Phoca sibirica

Family: Phocidae

World population: 85,000

Distribution: Lake Baikal, Russia

Habitat: Fresh water

Size: Length: 3.6–4.6 ft (1–1.4 m). Weight: 110–286 lb (50–130 kg)

Form: Small seal with relatively large front flippers; fur is dark gray-brown on back, paler beneath; pups have creamy-white coats

Diet: Freshwater fish; invertebrates

Breeding: Single young (sometimes twins), born February–March after 9-month gestation; weaned at 8.5–11 weeks; females mature at 6 years, males at 7 years. May live up to 56 years

Related endangered species: Baltic gray seal (*Halichooerus grypus*) EN; Mediterranean monk seal (*Monachus monachus*)* CR; Hawaiian monk seal (*M. schauinslandi*)* EN; Caspian seal (*Phoca caspica*) VU

Status: IUCN LRnt; not listed by CITES

RUSSIA
Lake Baikal
MONGOLIA
CHINA

See also: Pesticides 1: 51; Money Problems 1: 88; seal species 8: 72–79

probably accounts for an additional 2,000 to 4,000 seal deaths every year. Since most hunting happens in the northern parts of the lake, the seals are tending to breed farther south. However, temperatures in the south are warmer than those in the north, and the snow lairs in which the young are born melt earlier, leaving the pups exposed to bad weather and predators, including brown bears and large crows.

To add to the seal's difficulties, the waters in which they feed are highly polluted. Chemicals from industry—as well as pesticides, including the notorious DDT—pour into the lake and accumulate in the bodies of invertebrates, fish, and seals. Mother seals inevitably pass on large doses of pollutants to their young, both in the womb and through their milk. There is no doubt that pollution is at least partly responsible for a doubling of the infant death rate in recent years. The effects on older seals include failure to breed and weakened immunity to disease. In 1988 some 5,000 Baikal seals died from a form of distemper virus, and in the late 1990s there were hundreds of unexplained seal deaths suspiciously close to industrial sites on the lake shore.

Crisis Point

Lake Baikal has been made a World Heritage Site and includes several nature reserves and national parks. In theory the Baikal seals should also be protected, but in practice little is done. Indeed, one national park was so short of money that wardens were asked to help raise funds by leading trophy hunters on expeditions to shoot seals. The majority of seals that die each year are young. As a result, the main population consists of elderly animals; while older seals die or become infertile, fewer young healthy ones are starting to breed. The scale of the crisis for the Baikal seal is only just being realized. The hunting quota for the year 2000 was reduced to 3,500, and the health of the population is now being closely monitored. However, tackling the many and varied causes of the seals' decline will be costly and difficult.

Baikal seals *are descendants of seals that arrived sometime during the last ice age, when Lake Baikal was connected to the Arctic Ocean. Ice is still a factor in the lake, and it forces the seals to migrate north in spring and south in the fall, in much the same way as their ocean-going cousins.*

Seal, Gray

Halichoerus grypus

The gray seal is endangered in one part of its range. Elsewhere, it is regarded by some as a significant pest and risks large-scale culling to reduce numbers.

Populations of gray seal are spread across the Northern Hemisphere. There are about 5,000 individuals living in the semifresh waters of the Baltic area, where their numbers are in steady decline. This Baltic population is listed by the IUCN as Endangered; elsewhere populations are healthier.

About 75 percent of the eastern Atlantic population of gray seals are based in British waters. Large breeding colonies occur on some Hebridean and Orkney islands (off Scotland), and gray seals are found along the coasts of Wales and northern England.

Previously hunted for their skins, the species is now legally protected. An increase in numbers has brought gray seals into conflict with the fishing industry in parts of their range. In the 1960s fishermen claimed that seals were damaging their nets, causing significant economic losses. However, replacing old nets with new ones made of stronger material reduced the problem. It was also reported that seals would take bites out of the fish inside nets.

Controversial Culling

The apparent competition for fish resulted in calls from the fishing community for seal numbers to be reduced. The most effective method was to kill mothers and their pups on the breeding beaches. There was much public opposition, not least because the gray seal is one of the world's less abundant species. It was also recognized among experts that many male seals, prevented from coming ashore by the territorial bulls already in residence, would escape the cull. Instead of reducing the damage caused by

Gray seals *are the largest members of the true seal family. In the fall they come ashore to breed in large colonies, often on islands where they will be free from disturbance.*

DATA PANEL

Gray seal

Halichoerus grypus

Family: Phocidae

World population: About 200,000

Distribution: British and Scandinavian coasts; Iceland and Baltic area. Off Labrador and Nova Scotia; occasionally south to New Jersey

Habitat: Rocky coasts with sandy beaches; open sea

Size: Length head/body: males up to 10.8 ft (3.3 m); females 8.2 ft (2.5 m); tail: 4 in (10 cm). Weight: males up to 680 lb (310 kg); females up to 410 lb (186 kg)

Form: Large seal with dark-gray coat flecked with pale blotches. Top of head forms flat profile; snout is conical in bull

Diet: Fish; occasionally octopus

Breeding: Single young born per year; mature at about 4 years. Life span exceeds 40 years in females, lower for males

Related endangered species: Mediterranean monk seal *(Monachus monachus)** CR; Hawaiian monk seal *(M. schauinslandi)** EN; Caspian seal *(Phoca caspica)* VU. Several other seals have small, locally endangered populations

Status: IUCN (northeastern population) EN; not listed by CITES

See also: Why Are Mammals at Risk? **1:** 61; seal species **8:** 70–79

seals, culling would seriously disrupt the structure of the seal colonies. The issue was complicated further by the fact that the arguments in favor of seal culls may have been based on weak evidence. It is possible that the raiding of fishing nets was the work of a few rogue seals, and that killing large numbers would not have solved the problem. Seal deterrents on nets could well prove to be a more constructive approach.

In the 1970s seal numbers threatened to ruin the nesting areas used by puffins on the Farne Islands off the northeast coast of Britain. Both seals and puffins used the islands at different times of year. However, in winter the seals crushed puffin burrows and caused soil erosion, preventing the puffins from nesting successfully the following year. A seal cull began, but was called off after a public outcry. The solution found was to block the few routes from the beaches to the top of the islands, confining the seals to rocky shores.

Recently, gray seals have again been accused of depriving fishermen of their livelihoods. However, detailed research has demonstrated that the seals actually eat a lot of noncommercial species, thinning out smaller fish and leaving more food for commercially important species. In Germany a scare began after a television investigation into the seal worm, a parasite shared by seals and fish, and people were put off buying fish. Again, seal culls were proposed, although there was no evidence that reducing the number of seals would reduce the number of parasites.

Today the gray seal is under private attack by fish-farmers who use the sheltered waters of sea lochs to raise salmon in cages. Seals are attracted to the captive salmon and may damage the cages and eat their contents. Many seals are shot illegally if they are found raiding the cages.

Seal, Hawaiian Monk

Monachus schauinslandi

Until the Hawaiian Islands were colonized by humans, monk seals bred on most of the islands and atolls, taking advantage of the predator-free beaches to rear their pups. Today the story is different.

The Hawaiian monk seal's range started to contract when the main islands of Hawaii were colonized by Polynesians in AD 400. For a time monk seals still thrived on the smaller atolls and islands in the north of the archipelago, where they were rarely disturbed. However, it was not long before even these remote islands were also discovered, and the seal's situation deteriorated rapidly.

Despite living in warm, tropical seas, the Hawaiian monk seal has fur as luxurious as that of other seals. In the early 19th century hunters killed so many Hawaiian seals that by 1824 the species was thought to be extinct. In fact, small breeding populations had survived on some of the more remote Hawaiian islands. When such groups were discovered however, they too soon became prey to hunters.

Along with hunting, the mere presence of humans has also affected monk seal populations. The animals are extremely sensitive to disturbance, especially during the spring, when females give birth on sandy beaches. Under ideal circumstances the pups are born at the top of the beach, well above the high-tide mark and in the shelter of beachside vegetation. However, if the seal's traditional breeding sites are disturbed, expectant mothers may choose less suitable places to deliver, such as on remote sandy spits, from which a newborn seal can be washed away by a large wave or heavy seas. Even if the female has managed to give birth to her pup in a secure spot, she is quick to abandon it at the first sign of disturbance, leaving the youngster to starve. In the 1950s a study on the survival rates of young monk seals reported

DATA PANEL

Hawaiian monk seal

Monachus schauinslandi

Family: Phocidae

World population: About 1,300

Distribution: Mostly restricted to the Leeward Islands north of Hawaii

Habitat: Shallow lagoons and sandy beaches

Size: Length: 6.6–8.2 ft (2–2.5 m); females around 10% longer than males. Weight: 330–660 lb (150–300 kg); females heavier than males

Form: Dark-gray seal with velvety fur, silvery on underside; face has long, dark whiskers

Diet: Reef fish and invertebrates, especially eels and octopuses

Breeding: Single pup born every 1 or 2 years, usually between March and May; weaned at 6 weeks; mature at 5–6 years. May live as long as 30 years

Related endangered species: Mediterranean monk seal *(Monachus monachus)** CR; Caribbean monk seal *(M. tropicalis)* EX (last seen in 1952)

Status: IUCN EN; CITES I

See also: Organizations 1: 10; Tourism 1: 42; Pollution 1: 50; seal species 8: 70–79

that of all the pups born on a particular stretch of coast, 39 percent died before they reached the sea.

As more Hawaiian islands were exploited in the 20th century, the monk seals retreated. In 1978 up to 60 seals on Laysan Island died suddenly from a form of food poisoning known as ciguatera. The seals had eaten prey contaminated with a single-celled organism that produces a potent toxin. Such an event might seem like a natural hazard of a seafood diet, but it is now accepted that outbreaks of ciguatera are nearly always associated with damage to coral reefs. The incident was probably triggered by destruction of the reef during work on the harbor around Midway Atoll.

Generations of Hawaiians have made their living from the sea, and today commercial fisheries pose yet another threat to the seals. Every year seals are killed accidentally or deliberately: Debris, oil, and diesel spilled from all kinds of ships present a problem for the seals and other endangered wildlife, and many drown after becoming entangled in fishing nets.

Monk seals *have lived on the remote island paradise of Hawaii for about 15 million years. In that time seals in other parts of the world have evolved and adapted, while the isolated Hawaiian population has hardly changed at all.*

A More Secure Future

In 1980 the United States Fish and Wildlife Service took action. A monk-seal recovery team was formed to safeguard the remaining population. Today the entire breeding range of the Hawaiian monk seal falls within a specially designated national wildlife refuge, and the seals are strictly protected. A feature of the population is that there are three times as many males as females. Competition among the males is intense: Sometimes newborn pups are crushed or females killed by excited bull seals. In a small population such losses are significant. By removing some of the males, and giving others a testosterone-inhibiting drug to dampen aggressive behavior, the recovery team hopes to give the population a more secure future.

Seal, Mediterranean Monk

Monachus monachus

Although the monk seals of the Mediterranean are no longer hunted, they are extremely sensitive to disturbance of any kind. As many tourists know, undisturbed beaches in the Mediterranean are now few and far between.

The Greek philosopher and scientist Aristotle made the first scientific record of a seal in the 3rd century B.C. Since the Mediterranean monk is the only seal to inhabit the waters off southern Europe, there is little doubt that it was the species to which he referred. Ancient place names derived from the Greek word *phoca,* meaning seal, occur throughout Greece and Turkey, suggesting that the seals were once widespread in the region.

A few Mediterranean monk seals also live outside the Mediterranean. In fact, one of the largest remaining populations occurs in the tropical waters of Cap Blanc on the coast of Mauritania in northwestern Africa. One of the most remote and vulnerable populations lives around the Desertas Islands, a small group of rocky islets off Madeira. In 1989 that population contained just 10 individuals.

Environmental Disturbance

In more recent times the main hazard facing Mediterranean monk seal populations has come from environmental disturbance; the region's fishing and tourism industries are mostly to blame. Early records suggest that the seals used to pup on wide, sandy beaches, like those favored by their relative the Hawaiian monk seal. Yet today the same beaches are lined with hotels and visited by sunbathers and yachts. Consequently, the sensitive seals now rarely breed away from secluded coves surrounded by high cliffs, which are inaccessible to people. Most seals choose the even greater security of sea caves that can only be reached through underwater entrance tunnels.

Pregnant females are especially sensitive to disturbance, and even fairly minor incidents can cause them to miscarry. Although they are physiologically capable of having one young every year, in reality they rarely do so, and the overall reproduction rate is relatively low.

Another serious problem for the remaining scattered populations is competition with fishermen. The Mediterranean is one of the most intensively fished areas of water in the world. Humans and seals have similar tastes in seafood, including fish, octopus, and squid. Fishermen are none too willing to share their catch, and the seals make themselves very unpopular when they tear holes in the

---

DATA PANEL

Mediterranean monk seal

Monachus monachus

Family: Phocidae

World population: About 500

Distribution: Scattered populations around the Mediterranean and on the Atlantic coast of Mauritania in northwestern Africa

Habitat: Sheltered subtropical coast; small beaches and sea caves

Size: Length: 7.5–9.2 ft (2.3–2.8 m). Weight: 550–660 lb (250–300 kg)

Form: Large seal with short, dark, variably patterned coat; pale patch on belly

Diet: Fish, octopus, and squid

Breeding: Single pup born May–November after gestation of 9–10 months; weaned at 6 weeks but stays with mother for 3 years; mature at 4 years. May live up to 23 years

Related endangered species: Hawaiian monk seal (*Monachus shauinslandi*)* EN; Caribbean monk seal (*M. tropicalis*) EX

Status: IUCN CR; CITES I

See also: Tourism 1: 42; Natural Disasters 1: 57; seal species 8: 70–79

Mediterranean monk seals *basking on the rocks have been linked to the ancient Greek myth of the Sirens. The story goes that these deadly sea nymphs lured seamen onto the rocks with their beautiful singing.*

nets and make off with the contents. They regularly become entangled in the nets and, unable to return to the surface to breathe, drown in minutes.

It is largely as a result of centuries of hunting and habitat disturbance that the Mediterranean monk seal is now one of the world's rarest mammals. The sealing industry in the Mediterranean reached its peak in the 15th century; but even after hunting went into decline, the seal population continued to fall.

Still At Risk

The remaining Mediterranean monk seals are spread over a wide geographical area, and efforts to save them require determined international cooperation. The Greek population is now relatively secure; its breeding sites are protected within the Northern Sporades Marine Park. An intensive program of education, along with compensation for fishermen whose nets are damaged by seals, should mean that persecution is a thing of the past. However, even with protection, populations are now so small that they are increasingly vulnerable to natural hazards. In 1978 a sea cave at Cap Blanc collapsed on a breeding colony, killing up to 50 seals. Such natural disasters could harm almost any population of large mammals, but for a population of fewer than 300 it was devastating. Until the Mediterranean monk seal population is large enough to survive such incidents, it will remain one of the world's most critically endangered species.

Seal, Northern Fur

Callorhinus ursinus

Once abundant, the northern fur seal was commercially harvested under international agreement. Recently, numbers have fallen dramatically for reasons that are not understood.

Northern fur seals live in the north Pacific between Kamchatka (Siberia) and Alaska. There was once thought to be a total of about 4 million, but uncontrolled hunting reduced their numbers severely. Their thick, densely furred skin was highly prized for warm garments, and specially prepared furs were at one time very fashionable.

In the past hunters would shoot large numbers of northern fur seals out at sea. Not only was the method cruel, it was also extremely wasteful: Many seals were wounded, and the bodies were never recovered. Hunters soon discovered that it was easier—and more efficient—to kill the animals on the beaches where, for eight weeks of the year, they come ashore to breed.

Northern fur seals breed on the Pribilof Islands (off Alaska) and the Commander Islands (off Siberia), and previously were also found in small numbers on Japanese territory. Each year they migrate to the gloomy, rain-soaked shores, traveling up to 6,200 miles (10,000 km) to breed. Between 1867 and 1911 more than 1 million were taken, with at least as many again being killed and lost at sea.

It has proved extremely difficult to protect wildlife living in international waters. Attempts to control exploitation of seals in the early 20th century failed, and the population dwindled; some colonies died out altogether. In 1911 it was agreed to make the killing of fur seals illegal everywhere except the Pribilof colonies, which were tightly controlled by the United States. The American government managed the herds and shared the proceeds with its partner nations. The strategy seemed to work well. From a low point of fewer than 250,000 animals, the population grew to over 3 million by 1940. The increase occurred despite an annual harvest of about 40,000 seals.

DATA PANEL

Northern fur seal

Callorhinus ursinus

Family: Otariidae

World population: About 1 million

Distribution: North Pacific coasts as far south as California; main breeding on Pribilof Islands off Alaska and Commander Islands off Siberia

Habitat: Open sea within 60 miles (100 km) of the coast; comes ashore to rocky beaches to breed

Size: Length: male up to 6.5 ft (2.1 m); female up to 4.6 ft (1.2–1.5 m). Weight: male 300–615 lb (136–279 kg); female 66–110 lb (30–50 kg)

Form: A large fur seal; bulls reddish brown and black, cows pale and gray

Diet: Mainly fish

Breeding: One young born per year; mature from about 4 years. Life span probably more than 30 years

Related endangered species: Steller's sea lion (*Eumetopias jubatus*)* EN; Galápagos fur seal (*Arctocephalus galapagoensis*) VU; Juan Fernandez fur seal (*A. philippii*) VU; Guadaloupe fur seal (*A. townsendi*) VU

Status: IUCN VU; not listed by CITES

See also: Life Strategies 1: 24; Sea Lion, Steller's 8: 62; seal species 8: 70–77

Conservation Success

By the mid-20th century the case of the fur seal had become an example of successful conservation management combined with sustainable harvesting of animals in the wild. The harvesting, or culling, was possible because the northern fur seal is a harem breeder. The adult bulls come ashore in early summer and defend a breeding territory, keeping younger males at bay. Each "master" bull then has up to 100 females (cows) to himself, each of which is only a quarter of his size. This is the greatest male–female size difference of any mammal.

Only a small proportion of male fur seals ever breeds. The rest are kept away from the breeding beaches by the territorial bulls and can be found gathered together nearby in all-male groups. Many of the surplus males can therefore be killed with virtually no effect on the breeding population. The culling may even benefit the rest of the population by making more food available to those that are left, including females and young.

Unaccountable Decline

The harvest was managed in this way until 1984, the year when commercial hunting stopped. Although seals are now protected and no longer culled, their numbers have been in decline for many years: The main breeding population has halved in fewer than 50 years. Records show that about 50,000 seals drown in fishing nets each year, although this is not enough to account for the long-term decline. One explanation may be that overfishing has reduced the seal's food supply to a level that cannot support the previous numbers of seals.

There is better news from the Russian colonies, where fur seal numbers have held up: Some groups have recently recolonized Robben Island in the Sea of Okhotsk. About 4,000 animals have also begun to breed on San Miguel Island off southern California.

Northern fur seals *come ashore to rocky beaches to breed. Harems of between 40 and 100 females are dominated by one adult bull. An adult bull (below) has a heavy mane and a darker brown body than a cow.*

Shark, Basking

Cetorhinus maximus

The basking shark is a true giant of the oceans and the second largest living fish after the whale shark. Although it was first described in 1765, little is known about its way of life. However, activities such as commercial fishing have caused populations to decline.

Concern for the basking shark has gradually been increasing. Although population estimates vary, all point to the fact that the species has been experiencing a serious decline. Reported sightings around the Isle of Man off the coast of Britain, for example, dropped by about 85 percent over a seven-year period. Some years ago the basking shark was classified by the IUCN as Insufficiently Known, but some populations have now declined to the stage where they are listed as Endangered, while the species as a whole is now considered Vulnerable.

The continuation of the basking shark fishery (fish industry) in a number of countries, including Norway, China, and Japan, is controversial. According to a study carried out by the British-based Basking Shark Project, as many as 95 percent of all basking sharks taken by commercial fisheries are female. This is not the result of intentionally selective fishing, but a direct consequence of the fact that for unknown reasons the majority of basking sharks found feeding at the water surface are females. The removal of females from a population is, of course, bound to be detrimental.

Elusive Fish

It is surprising that we have so little understanding of a species that has been known about for some 250 years. Debate surrounds even basic data, such as the size attained by basking sharks. Although a length of 33 feet (10 m) is usually quoted, unconfirmed reports quote 45 feet (14 m); in 1948 a basking shark measuring 50.5 feet (15.4 m) was reported.

It is estimated that sexual maturity is reached at between two and four years old. Basking sharks can be aged by looking at the growth rings present in the individual bones of the vertebral column (like annual rings in trees). Some authorities believe that two rings are laid down each year,

DATA PANEL

Basking shark

Cetorhinus maximus

Family: Cetorhinidae

World population: Unknown, but now declining

Distribution: Temperate coastal regions of Pacific Ocean from British Columbia to Baja California, Australia, New Zealand, and up coast of Asia past Japan. In the Atlantic Ocean it is found from Newfoundland to South America, not including the Caribbean, and from Scandinavia to southern Africa. Also in the Mediterranean and Black Seas and the eastern Indian Ocean

Habitat: Surface waters, inshore and offshore, but probably also deeper zones (although no direct observations have been carried out)

Size: Length: 33 ft (10 m); maximum: 50.5 ft (15.4 m). Weight: up to 9.5 tons (8.6 tonnes)

Form: Brown or dusky black or blue along back, lighter toward dull-white belly. Pointed snout. Skin covered in small denticles (type of scale) and thick layer of mucus. Five large gill slits house food-filtering gill rakers. Caudal (tail) fin is typically shark-shaped with upper lobe longer than lower one

Diet: Planktonic invertebrates

Breeding: Poorly known. Internal fertilization; gestation about 3.5 years; Gives birth to 1 or 2 pups measuring about 5.5 ft (1.7 m). (Some estimates indicate maximum of 50 young in single batch.) Developing embryos believed to feed on unfertilized eggs. Life span 12–17 years

Related endangered species: Whale shark (*Rhincodon typus*)* VU

Status: IUCN VU (North Pacific population EN); CITES III

See also: Life Strategies 1: 24; Hunting 1: 42; Shark, Great White 8: 82; Shark, Whale 8: 87

and the number of rings is known to decrease as one moves down the vertebral column. However, estimates of age may turn out to be only approximate.

Mating takes place during the summer months in northern European waters and off Iceland. Afterward the females disappear. Fertilization is known to be internal, and the females are believed to incubate a small number of eggs within their bodies up to the moment of birth.

Commercial Uses

In the past the main product of commercial fishing of basking shark was squalene, an oil extracted from the shark's liver. As much as 75 percent of the liver consists of this oil: An adult basking shark liver can yield about 1,100 pounds (500 kg) of squalene. The high-quality oil was used mainly as a lubricant in aircraft engines, especially in high-flying planes. It was also used for lighting, but was eventually replaced. Other uses include squalene capsules as a dietary (vitamin) supplement and as an ingredient in skin moisturizers. In recent years research has indicated that squalene may have anticarcinogenic properties, which could lead to continuing demand for the oil.

In the early days of basking shark fishery the meat was eaten and the tough skin tanned for leather; both

Basking sharks *consume only microscopic plankton, despite their enormous size. According to the Basking Shark Project, a volume of water equivalent to that held by a 165-foot (50-m) swimming pool can be filtered every hour.*

industries have declined. However, the demand for the fins for Far Eastern markets remains, with 2 pounds (1 kg) of dried fins fetching up to $700.

Protective Measures

While there is not a universal protection program for basking sharks, several national and regional incentives are in place. The species has been protected since the mid-1990s in British waters, and New Zealand banned all target fishing for the species in 1991.

Unfortunately, such efforts to protect the species can only be marginally effective in global terms, since they apply only to national waters. Any sharks that move into international waters—outside the traditional 12-mile (19-km) limit—lose the protection and can be fished. So, despite a reduction in demand for basking shark "products," the need for protection remains.

Shark, Great White

Carcharodon carcharias

The great white shark is a hunter par excellence. It frequents a wide range of habitats, and within its domain its success is matched only by that other major predator, the orca, or killer whale.

The great white shark is magnificently designed. Torpedo-shaped and armed with multiple rows of replaceable saw-edged triangular teeth, it also has a battery of receptors that almost defy human comprehension. It can sense its prey from distances of over 1 mile (1.6 km); low-frequency sound waves can be picked up from this distance by the shark's ears, while low-frequency vibrations in the water are detected by its hypersensitive lateral line system (a system of sensory organs that detect even the slightest pressure changes and vibrations).

In addition to its long-distance senses the shark has an acute ability to detect weak electrical fields, such as those emitted by fish and other prey. The tiny pulses of electricity are picked up by the ends of ducts (ampullae of Lorenzini) located on the shark's snout. Such is the sensitivity of the ampullae that some sharks can locate prey such as flatfish even if it is buried in the sand.

Sharks can also sense blood—the unmistakable "signal" sent out by injured prey—at extremely weak dilutions. In experiments to find out more about the shark's capacity to detect weak solutions, lemon sharks were shown to sense tuna remnants or "juice" at an incredibly weak dilution of one part juice to 25 million parts of water.

The shark's ability to detect movement in dim light is aided by a membranous reflecting layer of cells located under the retina in the eye. It acts as a mirror, reflecting rays back through the retina, reactivating the light-sensitive cells in the process, and thus optimizing the eye's ability to detect movement in even minimal levels of illumination. This exceptional

---

DATA PANEL

Great white shark

Carcharodon carcharias

Family: Lamnidae

World population: About 10,000

Distribution: Worldwide, but predominantly in warm-temperate and subtropical waters; may also be found in warmer areas. Only infrequently encountered in cold northern regions

Habitat: Wide range of habitats from surf line to offshore (rarely in mid-ocean). Found between the surface and depths of 820 ft (250 m) or more

Size: Unconfirmed reports refer to specimens in excess of 23 ft (7 m). Confirmed data, however, indicates a maximum size of 18–20 ft (5.5–6 m)

Form: Torpedo-shaped fish with saw-edged triangular teeth. System of sensory organs for detecting prey; light-sensitive membrane below retina for tracking movement in dim light

Diet: Mainly bony fish but also cartilaginous fish (including other sharks); marine mammals, including cetaceans (whales and dolphins) and pinnipeds (seals and sea lions)

Breeding: Gives birth to 5–10 live young (probably more) after a gestation period that could last as long as 1 year

Related endangered species: Whale shark *(Rhincodon typus)** VU

Status: IUCN VU; not listed by CITES

See also: Populations **1:** 20; Shark, Basking **8:** 80; Shark, Whale **8:** 86

sensory system, combined with the other attributes possessed by sharks, has ensured their survival for over 200 million years.

Pressure from Humans

Exploitation by humans has taken its toll over the years. Direct killing for the entertainment of professional anglers or to obtain shark products for the souvenir trade has caused significant decline. Passive killing, with great white sharks being caught in nets set out for other target species, has also exerted pressure on populations, as have shark nets installed to protect bathers along shark-threatened coastlines.

The combined effects of these and other threats have led to a significant decline in great white shark numbers. The actual extent of this decline and the total number of great whites that remain in the wild are difficult to quantify. There are several reasons for this, including the diversity of nomadic and homing habits exhibited by the species. Some specimens, for

The great white shark *is an aggressive sea predator with a finely tuned sensory system. However, hunting and accidental killings by humans have taken their toll on population numbers.*

instance, tend to frequent relatively localized "territories," while others are known to roam over large distances. Another complicating factor is that, worldwide, the species is relatively scarce.

As a result, although a figure of 10,000 has been cited as a global total, it can only be approximate. Concerned by the decline, several countries have implemented protection programs. Measures range from banning all great white shark products to prohibiting activities such as fishing or underwater viewing by tourists. Further action is being urged by conservation bodies who fear that the current IUCN listing as Vulnerable may be incorrect and that the great white shark may already be Endangered.

Shark, Silver

Balantiocheilos melanopterus

Despite its name and a passing visual similarity to true sharks, the silver shark could not really be more different from its namesakes. It is not ferocious, it lacks true teeth, and it feeds on tiny insects and plants, rather than fish, squid, and other marine animals.

The silver shark is a popular aquarium fish. Ever since it was first imported into Europe in 1955, it has been in great demand worldwide, in particular the very attractively colored juveniles.

Shark Appeal

The label "shark" made the fish appealing to millions of aquarium keepers around the world, even though the freshwater aquarium fish are not related to their predatory, marine namesakes. Although there are many other, smaller, more colorful aquarium species, the demand for silver sharks is high.

The silver shark is a cyprinid (a member of the family Cyprinidae). The family includes other "sharks"—the red-tailed black shark, the rainbow or ruby shark, and the black shark; all have a profile with only superficial resemblance to a true shark.

One of the reasons for the popularity of the silver shark and other freshwater aquarium "sharks" is the relative ease with which they can be kept. They do not have exacting dietary or water chemistry demands, and assuming that appropriately roomy accommodation can be provided, it is perfectly possible to keep such fish in peak condition until they die of old age (after several years). Modern aquarium technology and husbandry techniques mean that even fully mature specimens of silver shark, or even the larger black shark, can be kept.

Wild Populations Under Pressure

At one time the silver shark was so abundant throughout its range in Southeast Asia that it was regarded as a Category I species for home aquaria.

DATA PANEL

Silver shark (bala shark, tricolor shark)

Balantiocheilos melanopterus

Family: Cyprinidae

World population: Virtually extinct in some parts of the range but abundant in others

Distribution: Kalimantan (Borneo), Sumatra (Indonesia), Thailand, and peninsular Malaysia

Habitat: Flowing, oxygen-rich waters

Size: Up to 14 in (35 cm)

Form: Elongated fish with a passing resemblance to true sharks. Body almost entirely covered in silvery, highly reflective, scales. Pectoral (chest) fins uncolored, but others are golden yellow and black

Diet: Wide range of aquatic insects and other invertebrates; delicate submerged vegetation

Breeding: In the wild mass spawnings occur following migration to breeding grounds. Eggs are scattered among vegetation or over the substratum and abandoned by the spawners

Related endangered species: None

Status: IUCN EN; not listed by CITES

See also: Exploitation of Live Animals **1:** 49; Barb, Bandula **2:** 52; Ikan Temoleh **5:** 82

The term applies to species that are in demand and are collected or bred in large quantities for aquarists.

The fish stocks appeared to be inexhaustible; but, as in so many instances, they eventually proved not to be. Demand continued, and local populations became overfished, so the search expanded into unexploited areas, including spawning grounds. Harvests removed not only juveniles from a population, but also a percentage of the breeding adults that would normally replenish the numbers. Existing stocks were therefore placed under unsustainable pressure.

Further pressures came from deforestation, with the accompanying habitat alteration, deterioration in water quality, and siltation. Eventually, the silver shark became scarce in parts of its range within Kalimantan and Sumatra, and was virtually wiped out in others. Thailand populations, however, remained almost untouched, so the species as a whole was not depleted to a point beyond recovery. Today, however, the Thai populations are also believed to be declining.

In recent years the main cause of decline has not been collection from the wild; demand by aquarists for the silver shark is now met from captive-bred stocks. Wild populations still face an uncertain future, however, as a result of various factors, including habitat alteration, water deterioration caused by the use of chemicals, and the small-mesh nets used in fishing. The problems are being addressed, but it will be some time before the solutions can be assessed.

Silver sharks are members of the Cyprinidae family, which includes the food fish carp, roach, and tench; they are typically toothless fish with rounded, smooth-edged scales. The silver shark's scales are shiny and highly reflective.

Shark, Whale

Rhincodon typus

The whale shark is the largest living fish in the world. However, unlike many other shark species, it is harmless to humans, feeding mainly on plankton. Ironically, its approachability has contributed to its decline; it has always been easy prey for fishermen.

Mature specimens of the whale shark are about 39 feet (just over 12 m), but can reach a length of 59 feet (18 m). The whale shark's closest rival in terms of size is the basking shark, which is about 33 feet (10 m), but can reach a length of 50 feet (nearly 15 m).

While they are undoubtedly sharks in every aspect of their biology, neither the whale shark nor the basking shark fits the description of a vicious predator,

an image that is commonly associated with many sharks. Furthermore, unlike other shark species such as the tiger shark, blue shark, hammerhead shark, and the great white shark, the basking shark and whale shark have not been known to attack humans.

Whale sharks are sluggish animals and tend to swim close to the surface of the water. Like basking sharks, they feed on plankton, which they filter from the sea using gill rakers. (All other sharks feed on a variety of animals, including fish, squid, octopus, and other small sharks.)

Easy Prey

The whale shark's habit of forming large groups in certain areas of the world ensures that considerable numbers are seen by humans (including tourists, conservationists, and scientists). It may be that the whale shark's approachability—which makes it attractive to divers—has also played a significant role in raising people's awareness about its vulnerability and threatened survival. However, whale sharks have human predators, and local hunting has taken a severe toll on whale shark populations. For example, it is reported that as many as 1,000 whale

DATA PANEL

Whale shark

Rhincodon typus

Family: Rhincodontidae

World population: Unknown

Distribution: Atlantic, Indian, and Pacific Oceans

Habitat: Tropical and temperate waters, both inshore and deep sea

Size: Length: 39 ft (12 m); may grow to 59 ft (18 m)

Form: Whalelike shark with broad, flat head, truncated snout, and large mouth with small teeth. Grayish color, with patterns of light spots and stripes unique to each individual

Diet: Zooplankton, small fish, and other small animals

Breeding: Internal fertilization; female retains fertilized eggs, which hatch within her body; young measure 16–20 in (40–50 cm) at birth

Related endangered species: Basking shark (*Cetorhinus maximus*)* VU; great white shark (*Carcharodon carcharias*)* VU; porbeagle (*Lamna nasus*) VU; blacktip shark (*Carcharhinus limbatus*) VU; sandbar shark (*C. plumbeus*) LRnt; Ganges shark (*Glyphis gangeticus*) CR; bluntnose six-gill shark (*Hexanchus griseus*) LRnt; sand tiger shark (*Carcharias taurus*) VU; dusky shark (*C. obscurus*) VU; kitefin shark (*Dalatias licha*) DD

Status: IUCN VU; not listed by CITES

See also: Hunting **1:** 42; Research **1:** 84; Shark, Great White **8:** 82; Shark, Basking **8:** 80

sharks were killed by fishermen from just three Indian villages in one year. Statistics such as these immediately raise the question: Can the world population of whale sharks sustain such a level of hunting? No one knows whether there are separate populations of whale sharks or just one single, migratory world population. If there is only one population, then sustained removal at the level of 1,000 or more creatures a year will be extremely harmful to the species.

Limited Knowledge

Information about whale sharks is extremely limited. For example, no one knows how many whale sharks exist worldwide or details of their growth rate and life span. There are numerous other aspects of their biology that are not yet understood. Ironically, a lack of knowledge is one of the reasons that the whale

Despite their great size, *whale sharks are placid creatures, and divers can approach them safely. They are slow moving and tend to swim close to the surface of the water.*

shark has not been regarded as a commercially exploitable species.

Action is now being taken by several countries to gather information about the whale shark; at the same time, measures are being implemented to protect existing populations. Conservation programs have also been set up on the eastern seaboard of the United States, as well as in the Maldives, the Philippines, and Western Australia. It is hoped that data from the various projects can be used to help ensure the whale shark's survival. The expansion of such measures to include other regions used by whale sharks is another step in the right direction.

Sheep, Barbary

Ammotragus lervia

Barbary sheep were once widespread and common across the desert hills of North Africa, but their numbers have been seriously reduced. They may now be more secure in the southern United States, where they have been introduced and managed for recreational hunting.

Barbary sheep (or aoudad) live in small family herds dominated by a single adult male. The females give birth to a single lamb, or occasionally twins, in the spring. By remaining in small family parties, the wild sheep do not have a big effect on the sparse desert vegetation of their range. In contrast, the large herds of domestic sheep that are now common in many arid areas of North Africa stick together and eat almost everything. As a result, the vegetation becomes severely depleted, and the ground is exposed to the wind and blistering sun, causing serious soil erosion. The introduction of domestic sheep in place of wild ones has had serious consequences for whole ecosystems.

The Barbary sheep was once a common and successful species, spread across a wide area north of the Sahara Desert. There was also a separate population of the species living as far east as the Red Sea coast in Egypt, but this is now extinct. Sadly, the process of extinction is slowly overtaking the remaining populations across the rest of North Africa, reducing the number of places where the Barbary sheep still survive.

Diminishing Numbers

Expansion of human settlements over many centuries has forced the Barbary sheep out of its natural range, leaving small groups, often separated by hundreds of miles. Isolated populations are vulnerable to extinction as a result of chance events, such as the failure of desert rains. Small populations are also in danger of inbreeding, because they are too far from other groups to mix successfully.

DATA PANEL

Barbary sheep (aoudad)

Ammotragus lervia

Family: Bovidae

World population: Low thousands, but many of them in semicaptivity

Distribution: Highlands in the Sahara, from central Mauritania to the Hamra plateau in Libya and from Algeria/Niger border to Darfur in western Sudan. Semicaptive introduced populations in Texas and New Mexico

Habitat: Desert, among sparse vegetation

Size: Length: 4.3–5.5 ft (1.3–1.5 m); height at shoulder: 2.5–3.7 ft (0.75–1 m). Weight: 110–220 lb (50–100 kg); males up to 264 lb (120 kg)

Form: Sturdy, pale-brown animal; resembles hybrid sheep-goat. Both sexes have fringe of long hair down throat, almost reaching ground in some males; shaggy hair on upper part of forelegs. Face long and pointed with white around muzzle. Horns in both sexes; much longer in males

Diet: Grass, flowers, and shrubs, varying seasonally. Can survive long periods without water

Breeding: Breeds September–November. One young, occasionally twins, born in spring after 6-month gestation. Life span 5–10 years

Related endangered species: Markhor *(Capra falconeri)** EN

Status: IUCN VU; CITES II

See also: Communities and Ecosystems **1:** 22; Pasture **1:** 38; Hunting **1:** 42; Ibex, Nubian **5:** 70; Markhor **6:** 72

In the past many Barbary sheep were killed by hunters using dogs. More recently (and more effectively) modern rifles have been used to kill large numbers of animals. The skins are valued by desert people and are used in making soft leather slippers and for other domestic purposes. The meat is highly prized and has been sold in the markets of Algeria and Morocco for over 100 years. Since the 1950s the Sahara region has seen an influx of soldiers and oil workers who have settled in the area. They have money, weapons, and helicopters that they use to hunt the animals, seeking them out even in the most remote areas where they would once have been safe. However, the major cause of the Barbary sheep's decline has been the steadily increasing numbers of domestic sheep and goats kept by desert people, which eat the already scarce foodstuffs of the arid desert.

Survival as Game

The wild populations of Barbary sheep in Africa are now small, widely scattered, and everywhere vulnerable to further losses. For over 200 years they have bred well in zoos and wildlife parks, so there are plenty of Barbary sheep in captivity. In the 1950s some surplus animals from zoos were released onto game ranches in Texas and New Mexico. The sheep are kept there as a novelty for hunters to shoot and collect as trophies. We might not like the idea of keeping rare animals for the entertainment of hunters, but it is now unlikely that the wild and semicaptive populations in America will die out completely. Ironically, the Barbary sheep thrives in the United States for the purposes of human recreation, but its future as a wild animal in Africa is uncertain.

The Barbary sheep
has a distinctive shaggy mane and long muzzle. It is becoming rare in its African homeland, but semiwild populations have been established in Texas and New Mexico.

Shrew, Giant Otter

Potamogale velox

The giant otter shrew occupies a large range in Central Africa. Nevertheless, it is poorly known, and its future is blighted by hunting, deforestation, pollution, and general lawlessness in areas of political instability.

The three species of otter shrew living in Africa are the only mainland members of the tenrec family, which is otherwise found exclusively on the island of Madagascar. Tenrecs were among the first mammals to colonize Madagascar from mainland Africa. For many thousands of years they had the place to themselves, and they diversified into an extraordinary range of forms and habits.

However, the mainland cousins of these early mammalian pioneers did not have it quite so easy. With other kinds of mammals already occupying niches in Africa's diverse habitats, they had to find alternative specializations in order to survive. The mainland otter shrews have evolved so much and become so different to the Malagasy branch of the family that some zoologists place them in a separate family of their own. Two small species live in tiny areas of West Africa and Uganda, but the giant otter shrew occurs widely across Central Africa.

Coveted Creatures

The giant otter shrew is one of the world's largest aquatic insectivores, almost as big as a true otter. Its common name is an apt one, since its specialization to an aquatic lifestyle makes it look much like a small otter or mink. Like both otters and mink, the giant otter shrew has fine, dense fur. The hairs trap an insulating layer of air, giving the shrew a silvery appearance under the water and helping keep it warm—even in tropical Africa mountain streams can be chilly.

Unfortunately, the animal's splendid pelt is coveted by humans, and the giant otter shrew has been hunted for its skin in many parts of its range.

DATA PANEL

Giant otter shrew (giant African water shrew)

Potamogale velox

Family: Tenrecidae

World population: Unknown

Distribution: Central Africa, including Nigeria, Gabon, Cameroon, Central African Republic, Uganda, Kenya, Democratic Republic of Congo (formerly Zaire), Rwanda, Burundi, Tanzania, Zambia, and Angola

Habitat: Fast- and slow-moving streams from sea level to 5,900 ft (1,800 m)

Size: Length head/body: 11.5–14 in (29–35 cm); tail: 9.5–35 in (24.5–90 cm). Weight: 12–14 oz (340–400 g)

Form: Otterlike animal with cylindrical body, powerful tail, and short legs; fur short and dense, brown to black above, pale below; head has broad, flat snout with stiff whiskers, small eyes, and small ears

Diet: Freshwater crustaceans (mainly crabs); also mollusks, fish, insects, and amphibians

Breeding: Two litters of 1 or 2 young born at any time of year

Related endangered species: Nimba otter shrew (*Micropotamogale lamottei*) EN; pygmy otter shrew (*M. ruwenzorii*) EN; aquatic tenrec (*Limnogale mergulus*)* EN

Status: IUCN EN; not listed by CITES

See also: Habitat Loss **1:** 38; Saving the Habitats **1:** 88; Tenrec, Aquatic **9:** 64

While hunting is to be discouraged, the decline in giant otter shrew numbers probably has more to do with habitat destruction than with direct killing. The animals live in streams that pass through forested areas. They do not venture far from the water, and it is possible that they could survive with only a narrow strip of trees on either side of the watercourse. It would certainly cost the timber companies little to leave such areas alone when they cut down the rest of the forest. However, such narrow corridors of habitat are less useful to the majority of nonaquatic, forest-dwelling mammals, and most conservationists would prefer to see much larger areas of forest being protected so that other animals could also benefit.

Habitat Erosion

One of the side effects of deforestation is a dramatic increase in soil erosion. Soil and silt—no longer bound up by tree roots or protected and enriched by a layer of humus—are washed into streams and rivers every time it rains. In the wet season especially, a clear stream becomes a torrent of muddy water, and the effect is not limited to deforested areas. The mud is carried miles downstream, contaminating habitat that would otherwise still be suitable for otter shrews.

The giant otter shrew *has many of the characteristics of a true otter, including a powerful tail for swimming. It also has a flattened snout, with the nose, eyes, and ears near the top of the head, allowing it to see, hear and breathe with only a fraction of its head above water.*

The shrews have poor sight at the best of times and tend to rely more on scent and touch to find their prey. With the help of their other senses they are able to trap prey in cloudy water, even if visibility is reduced to zero. However, otter shrews can only hunt successfully if there is plenty of prey around. With mud and silt blocking out the sunlight, few aquatic plants can grow, so plant-eating stream creatures are scarce. The gills and filter-feeding mechanisms of fish and crustaceans become clogged, and they soon die off, leaving the otter shrews with nothing to eat.

There are no otter shrews in captivity, and nobody knows how many survive in the wild. However, the rapid destruction of their habitat by local and upstream deforestation means that they are facing a serious decline, and the situation is worsening.

91

Sifaka, Golden-Crowned

Propithecus tattersalli

The golden-crowned sifaka, a member of the lemur family, was only recognized as a separate species in 1988. It is now considered one of the world's most critically endangered primates.

There are three species of sifaka in Madagascar, each occupying a different part of the island. The golden-crowned sifaka was first noted by a zoologist in the early 1970s, when it was thought to be a subspecies of the diadem sifaka, which lives in the forests of eastern Madagascar. However, close inspection of the new variety revealed many significant differences, and in 1988 the golden-crowned sifaka was declared a species in its own right.

Scientists immediately tried to discover just how many golden-crowned sifakas there were. During a 2-mile (4-km) walk in the forest they saw 26 individuals—a number that could suggest that the animal is common. Indeed, the scientists concluded that there were probably between 130 and 150 golden-crowned sifakas occupying every square mile within their range. However, the range itself is very small—an isolated patch of forest no more than 15 miles (25 km) across. The land is not protected, and commercial timber cutting and slash-and-burn agriculture continue. There is a thriving gold-mining community in the middle of the sifaka's range, representing a further threat to the environment.

Life in the Trees

Thousands of years of evolution have equipped the sifakas for a life spent feeding on leaves and living in trees in small family groups. The animals move through the trees with great leaps and are alert and intelligent enough to evade many predators. They use a variety of sounds to communicate and warn of danger—the "sifaka" call after which they are named is used to alert others to an approaching ground predator. However, in the 2,000 years since humans first came to the island of Madagascar the sifakas have found their peaceful way of life under threat.

In the Name of Progress

Until relatively recently persecution of the sifakas was indirect. Malagasy folklore includes many traditional "fadys," or taboos, which warn against the killing of certain animals. While local people had no qualms about cutting down the forest, most obeyed tradition and did not deliberately kill the sifakas. However, some people were not so scrupulous, and today sifakas are in danger of being hunted for food. Malagasy law protects all lemurs, but the law is rarely enforced. The roads built to service mining activities on the island are making the forest more accessible to more people, including some who will hunt lemurs.

Sifakas breed slowly. Only one female in a group is allowed to mate, and even she is only able to have one baby at a time. In addition, females have just one opportunity a year to breed; if it is missed, or if the baby is lost, she can mate again only after a year.

There have been some attempts to breed the golden-crowned sifaka in captivity, but progress is slow. At present there are not enough sifakas living in captivity to sustain a viable breeding program. More animals could be taken from the wild, but the death rate among newly captured sifakas is very high. The only realistic conservation option is to restrict further development, declare the sifaka's range a national park, and strictly enforce the existing protective laws.

The golden-crowned sifaka, *like its close relative the indri, is at home in the trees, where it finds most of its food. As a result, it rarely comes down to the ground.*

See also: Life Strategies **1:** 24; Speciation **1:** 26; Indri **5:** 84

DATA PANEL

Golden-crowned sifaka (Tattersall's sifaka)

Propithecus tattersalli

Family: Indridae

World population: A few hundred (pre-1990 estimate)

Distribution: Northeastern Madagascar

Habitat: Deciduous and evergreen forest

Size: Length head/body: 18–22 in (45–55 cm); tail: 17–22 in (43–56 cm). Weight: 6.5–15.5 lb (3–7 kg)

Form: Long-legged lemur with long tail; deep, whitish fur; black hairless face; prominent furry ears; orange crown

Diet: Unripe fruit; seeds, leaves, flowers, and bark

Breeding: Single young born May–August after gestation of 4.5–6 months; weaned at 5–6 months; mature at 2–3 years. Life span unknown

Related endangered species: Diadem sifaka *(Propithecus diadema)* EN; Verreaux's sifaka *(P. verreauxi)* VU; indri *(Indri indri)** EN; avahi *(Avahi occidentalis)* VU

Status: IUCN CR; CITES I

Siskin, Red

Carduelis cucullata

The strikingly attractive red siskin has been brought to the verge of extinction chiefly as a result of the relentless demands of the cage-bird trade.

Until the early years of the 20th century the red siskin was common in northernmost South America. Once it could be found throughout the foothills of the mountain ranges of northern Venezuela at altitudes of between 900 and 4,250 feet (280 and 1,300 m); it was also found in northern Colombia. There was a very small population on the island of Trinidad, which originated either from birds taken there and deliberately introduced into the wild, or from cage birds that had escaped from captivity. The species was also introduced to Puerto Rico during the 1920s or 1930s, and the small numbers recorded in the wild in Cuba suggest that these birds had escaped from captivity on the island.

Today, by contrast, the red siskin is extremely rare and is restricted to a few fragments of its former range. While in the past it could be found in 15 different states in Venezuela, in recent years there have been only a few sightings from just four states. The only known population in Colombia is a small one in the state of Norte de Santander on the northeastern border with Venezuela. The Trinidad population has disappeared entirely, and there are very few recent records of the species from Puerto Rico.

Ruthless Trapping

The main reason for this little finch's catastrophic decline has been trapping for the cage-bird trade. Since the 1940s trade in the birds has been illegal, but trappers—who supplied a huge demand for red siskins—were not to be deterred. Trapping continued on a massive scale for much of the 20th century.

The demand was not so much for the intrinsic beauty of the birds themselves as for their use in interbreeding with domestic canaries. Breeders found that the red siskins were closely enough related to the domestic birds to attempt to introduce genes for red color into the domestic stock, thus producing the highly sought-after "red-factor canaries."

However, because domestic canaries belong to a different genus from that of the red siskin, breeders have found it difficult to transfer the "red" gene into canary stocks. Although they have bred types they call "red canaries," these birds have a reddish tinge rather than the splendid bright coloration of the red siskin.

DATA PANEL

Red siskin

Carduelis cucullata

Family: Fringillidae

World population: About 250–1,000 birds

Distribution: Recent sightings in 4 states in northern Venezuela; used to occur throughout foothills of north. Population in northern Colombia; population of escaped cage birds in Puerto Rico; another on Trinidad

Habitat: Moves seasonally and daily between moist evergreen forest, dry deciduous woodland, and adjacent shrubby grassland and pastureland

Size: Length: 4 in (10 cm)

Form: Small, brightly patterned red-and-black finch. Male has jet-black head, chin, throat, and tail; also black wings with broad red bar across flight feathers; rest of plumage rich scarlet to pinkish red. Female is brownish gray from head to back; crown, nape, and "shoulders" streaked darker; rump and wingbars bright orange-red

Diet: Seeds of trees and shrubs; grass seeds, flower heads, and cactus fruit

Breeding: Main nesting season May–early June; second breeding period in November and December. Builds neat, cup-shaped nest in tall trees

Related endangered species: Yellow-faced siskin (*Carduelis yarrellii*) VU; saffron siskin (*C. siemiradzkii*) VU; Warsangli linnet (*C. johannis*) EN

Status: IUCN EN; CITES I

In more recent years keepers of cage birds have shown more interest in the species for its own undeniable beauty. However, the trapping of wild birds did not stop, despite the species' rarity. In 1975 almost 3,000 red siskins were known to have been caught. Even in 1981, when total numbers were doubtless far fewer, just over 1,000 birds were still trapped. After breeding, the birds would gather in large flocks, which were easily lured to baits and caught; but recently only single birds or pairs have been seen.

As if this relentless trapping was not enough of a threat, red siskins also face loss of habitat as a result of the spread of intensive agriculture.

A Difficult Task

The task that lies ahead for conservationists trying to save the red siskin is not an easy one. Despite being legally protected in Venezuela and being listed on CITES Appendix I, trapping may still continue as a result of the difficulties of enforcing the law on the ground. There have been no records of the species for many years from the Venezuelan national parks of Guatopo and Terepaima— the only protected areas where the birds were reputed to have occurred.

Although captive-breeding programs have been initiated, they have been beset by problems of disease and genetically impure stock; a project to reintroduce the species to Trinidad had to be abandoned because of disease. Although there is a need to raise public awareness of the species' plight, some past education initiatives have had the opposite effect, leading to an increase in pressure from the cage-bird trade.

The red siskin has long been a target for cage-bird traders. Large numbers went to breeders intent on introducing the genes for red color—particularly prominent in the male (above)—into domestic canaries.

A major problem is that no one knows how many individuals there are left in the wild. Recent estimates vary from a few thousand to several hundred, but the true figure may not be known until it is so small that it is impossible to save the species in the wild.

95

Glossary

Words in SMALL CAPITALS refer to other entries in the glossary.

Adaptation features of an animal that adjust it to its environment; may be produced by evolution—e.g., camouflage-coloration

Adaptive radiation where a group of closely related animals (e.g., members of a FAMILY) have evolved differences from each other so that they can survive in different NICHES

Adhesive disks flattened disks on the tips of the fingers or toes of certain climbing AMPHIBIANS that enable them to cling to smooth, vertical surfaces

Adult a fully grown sexually mature animal; a bird in its final PLUMAGE

Algae primitive plants ranging from microscopic, single-celled forms to large forms, such as seaweeds, but lacking proper roots or leaves

Alpine living in mountainous areas, usually over 5,000 feet (1,500 m)

Ambient describing the conditions around an animal, e.g., the water temperature for a fish or the air temperature for a land animal

Amphibian any cold-blooded VERTEBRATE of the CLASS Amphibia, typically living on land but breathing in the water; e.g., frogs, toads, newts, salamanders

Amphibious able to live on both land and in water

Amphipod a type of CRUSTACEAN found on land and in both fresh and seawater

Anadromous fish that spend most of their life at sea but MIGRATE into fresh water for breeding, e.g., salmon

Annelid of the PHYLUM Annelida in which the body is made up of similar segments, e.g., earthworms, lugworms, leeches

Anterior the front part of an animal

Arachnid one of a group of ARTHROPODS of the CLASS Arachnida, characterized by simple eyes and four pairs of legs. Includes spiders and scorpions

Arboreal living in trees

Aristotle's lantern complex chewing apparatus of sea-urchins that includes five teeth

Arthropod the largest PHYLUM in the animal kingdom in terms of the number of SPECIES in it. Characterized by a hard, jointed EXOSKELETON and paired jointed legs. Includes INSECTS, spiders, crabs, etc.

Baleen horny substance commonly known as whalebone and growing as plates in the mouth of certain whales; used as a fringelike sieve for extracting plankton from seawater

Bill often called the beak: the jaws of a bird, consisting of two bony MANDIBLES, upper and lower, and their horny sheaths

Biodiversity the variety of SPECIES and the variation within them

Biome a major world landscape characterized by having similar plants and animals living in it, e.g., DESERT, jungle, forest

Biped any animal that walks on two legs. *See* QUADRUPED

Blowhole the nostril opening on the head of a whale through which it breathes

Breeding season the entire cycle of reproductive activity, from courtship, pair formation (and often establishment of territory) through nesting to independence of young

Bristle in birds a modified feather, with a bare or partly bare shaft, like a stiff hair; functions include protection, as with eyelashes of ostriches and hornbills, and touch sensors to help catch INSECTS, as with flycatchers

Brood the young hatching from a single CLUTCH of eggs

Browsing feeding on leaves of trees and shrubs

Cage bird A bird kept in captivity; in this set it usually refers to birds taken from the wild

Canine tooth a sharp stabbing tooth usually longer than the rest

Canopy continuous (closed) or broken (open) layer in forests produced by the intermingling of branches of trees

Carapace the upper part of a shell in a CHELONIAN

Carnivore meat-eating animal

Carrion rotting flesh of dead animals

Casque the raised portion on the head of certain REPTILES and birds

Catadromous fish that spend most of their life in fresh water but MIGRATE to the sea for SPAWNING, e.g., eels

Caudal fin the tail fin in fish

Cephalothorax a body region of CRUSTACEANS formed by the union of the head and THORAX. *See* PROSOMA

Chelicerae the first pair of appendages ("limbs") on the PROSOMA of spiders, scorpions, etc. Often equipped to inject venom

Chelonian any REPTILE of the ORDER Chelonia, including the tortoises and turtles, in which most of the body is enclosed in a bony capsule

Chrysalis the PUPA in moths and butterflies

Class a large TAXONOMIC group of related animals. MAMMALS, INSECTS, and REPTILES are all CLASSES of animals

Cloaca cavity in the pelvic region into which the alimentary canal, genital, and urinary ducts open

Cloud forest moist, high-altitude forest characterized by a dense UNDERSTORY and an abundance of ferns, mosses, and other plants growing on the trunks and branches of trees

Clutch a set of eggs laid by a female bird in a single breeding attempt

Cocoon the protective coat of many insect LARVAE before they develop into PUPAE or the silken covering secreted to protect the eggs

Colonial living together in a colony

Coniferous forest evergreen forests found in northern regions and mountainous areas, dominated by pines, spruce, and cedars

Costal riblike

Costal grooves grooves running around the body of some TERRESTRIAL salamanders; they conduct water from the ground to the upper parts of the body

Coverts small feathers covering the bases of a bird's main flight feathers on the wings and tail, providing a smooth, streamlined surface for flight

Crustacean member of a CLASS within the PHYLUM Arthropoda typified by five pairs of legs, two pairs of antennae, a joined head and THORAX, and calcerous deposits in the EXOSKELETON; e.g., crabs, shrimps, etc.

Deciduous forest dominated by trees that lose their leaves in winter (or in the dry season)

Deforestation the process of cutting down and removing trees for timber or to create open space for growing crops, grazing animals, etc.

Desert area of low rainfall typically with sparse scrub or grassland vegetation or lacking it altogether

Diatoms microscopic single-celled ALGAE

Dispersal the scattering of young animals going to live away from where they were born and brought up

Diurnal active during the day

DNA (deoxyribonucleic acid) the substance that makes up the main part of the chromosomes of all living things; contains the genetic code that is handed down from generation to generation

Domestication process of taming and breeding animals to provide help and useful products for humans

Dormancy a state in which—as a result of hormone action—growth is suspended and METABOLIC activity is reduced to a minimum

Dorsal relating to the back or spinal part of the body; usually the upper surface

Down soft, fluffy, insulating feathers with few or no shafts found after hatching on young birds and in ADULTS beneath the main feathers

Echolocation the process of perception based on reaction to the pattern of reflected sound waves (echos); occurs in bats

Ecology the study of plants and animals in relation to one another and to their surroundings

Ecosystem a whole system in which plants, animals, and their environment interact

Ectotherm animal that relies on external heat sources to raise body temperature; also known as "cold-blooded"

Edentate toothless; also any animals of the order Edentata, which includes anteaters, sloths, and armadillos

Endemic found only in one geographical area, nowhere else

Epitoke a form of marine ANNELID having particularly well developed swimming appendages

Estivation inactivity or greatly decreased activity during hot weather

Eutrophication an increase in the nutrient chemicals (nitrate, phosphate, etc.) in water, sometimes occurring naturally and sometimes caused by human activities, e.g., by the release of sewage or agricultural fertilizers

Exoskeleton a skeleton covering the outside of the body or situated in the skin, as found in some INVERTEBRATES

Explosive breeding in some AMPHIBIANS when breeding is completed over one or a very few days and nights

Extinction process of dying out at the end of which the very last individual dies, and the SPECIES is lost forever

Family a group of closely related SPECIES that often also look quite similar. Zoological FAMILY names always end in -idae. Also used to describe a social group within a SPECIES comprising parents and their offspring

Feral domestic animals that have gone wild and live independently of people

Flagship species A high-profile SPECIES, which (if present) is likely to be accompanied by many others that are typical of the habitat. (If a naval flagship is present, so is the rest of the fleet of warships and support vessels)

Fledging period the period between a young bird hatching and acquiring its first full set of feathers and being able to fly

Fledgling young bird that is capable of flight; in perching birds and some others it corresponds with the time of leaving the nest

Fluke either of the two lobes of the tail of a whale or related animal; also a type of flatworm, usually parasitic

Gamebird birds in the ORDER Galliformes (megapodes, cracids, grouse, partridges, quail, pheasants, and relatives); also used for any birds that may be legally hunted by humans

Gene the basic unit of heredity, enabling one generation to pass on characteristics to its offspring

Genus (genera, pl.) a group of closely related SPECIES

Gestation the period of pregnancy in MAMMALS, between fertilization of the egg and birth of the baby

Gill Respiratory organ that absorbs oxygen from the water. External gills occur in tadpoles. Internal gills occur in most fish

Harem a group of females living in the same territory and consorting with a single male

Hen any female bird

Herbivore an animal that eats plants (grazers and BROWSERS are herbivores)

Hermaphrodite an animal having both male and female reproductive organs

Herpetologist ZOOLOGIST who studies REPTILES and AMPHIBIANS

Hibernation becoming inactive in winter, with lowered body temperature to save energy. Hibernation takes place in a special nest or den called a hibernaculum

Homeotherm an animal that can maintain a high and constant body temperature by means of internal

processes; also called "warm-blooded"

Home range the area that an animal uses in the course of its normal activity

Hybrid offspring of two closely related SPECIES that can breed; it is sterile and so cannot produce offspring

Ichthyologist ZOOLOGIST specializing in the study of fish

Inbreeding breeding among closely related animals (e.g., cousins), leading to weakened genetic composition and reduced survival rates

Incubation the act of keeping the egg or eggs warm or the period from the laying of eggs to hatching

Indwellers ORGANISMS that live inside others, e.g., the California Bay pea crab, which lives in the tubes of some marine ANNELID worms, but do not act as PARASITES

Indigenous living naturally in a region; native (i.e., not an introduced SPECIES)

Insect any air-breathing ARTHROPOD of the CLASS Insecta, having a body divided into head, THORAX, and abdomen, three pairs of legs, and sometimes two pairs of wings

Insectivore animal that feeds on INSECTS. Also used as a group name for hedgehogs, shrews, moles, etc.

Interbreeding breeding between animals of different SPECIES, varieties, etc. within a single FAMILY or strain; Interbreeding can cause dilution of the GENE pool

Interspecific between SPECIES

Intraspecific between individuals of the same SPECIES

Invertebrates animals that have no backbone (or other bones) inside their body, e.g., mollusks, INSECTS, jellyfish, crabs

Iridescent displaying glossy colors produced (e.g., in bird PLUMAGE) not as a result of pigments but by the splitting of sunlight into light of different wavelengths; rainbows are made in the same way

Joey a young kangaroo living in its mother's pouch

Juvenile a young animal that has not yet reached breeding age

Keel a ridge along the CARAPACE of certain turtles or a ridge on the scales of some REPTILES

Keratin tough, fibrous material that forms hair, feathers, nails, and

protective plates on the skin of VERTEBRATE animals

Keystone species a SPECIES on which many other SPECIES are wholly or partially dependent

Krill PLANKTONIC shrimps

Labyrinth specialized auxiliary (extra) breathing organ found in some fish

Larva an immature form of an animal that develops into an ADULT form through METAMORPHOSIS

Lateral line system a system of pores running along a fish's body. These pores lead to nerve endings that allow a fish to sense vibrations in the water and help it locate prey, detect PREDATORS, avoid obstacles, and so on. Also found in AMPHIBIANS

Lek communal display area where male birds of some SPECIES gather to attract and mate with females

Livebearer animal that gives birth to fully developed young (usually refers to REPTILES or fish)

Mammal any animal of the CLASS Mammalia—warm-blooded VERTEBRATE having mammary glands in the female that produce milk with which it nurses its young. The class includes bats, primates, rodents, and whales

Mandible upper or lower part of a bird's beak or BILL; also the jawbone in VERTEBRATES; in INSECTS and other ARTHROPODS mandibles are mouth parts mostly used for biting and chewing

Mantle cavity a space in the body of mollusks that contains the breathing organs

Marine living in the sea

Matriarch senior female member of a social group

Metabolic rate the rate at which chemical activities occur within animals, including the exchange of gasses in respiration and the liberation of energy from food

Metamorphosis the transformation of a LARVA into an ADULT

Migration movement from one place to another and back again; usually seasonal

Molt the process in which a bird sheds its feathers and replaces them with new ones; some MAMMALS, REPTILES, and ARTHROPODS regularly molt, shedding hair, skin, or outer layers

Monotreme egg-laying MAMMAL, e.g., platypus

Montane in a mountain environment

Natural selection the process

whereby individuals with the most appropriate ADAPTATIONS are more successful than other individuals and therefore survive to produce more offspring. Natural selection is the main process driving evolution in which animals and plants are challenged by natural effects (such as predation and bad weather), resulting in survival of the fittest

Nematocyst the stinging part of animals such as jellyfish, usually found on the tentacles

Nestling a young bird still in the nest and dependent on its parents

New World the Americas

Niche part of a habitat occupied by an ORGANISM, defined in terms of all aspects of its lifestyle

Nocturnal active at night

Nomadic animals that have no fixed home, but wander continuously

Noseleaf fleshy structures around the face of bats; helps focus ULTRASOUNDS used for ECHOLOCATION

Ocelli markings on an animal's body that resemble eyes. Also, the tiny, simple eyes of some INSECTS, spiders, CRUSTACEANS, mollusks, etc.

Old World non-American continents

Olfaction sense of smell

Operculum a cover consisting of bony plates that covers the GILLS of fish

Omnivore an animal that eats a wide range of both animal and vegetable food

Order a subdivision of a CLASS of animals, consisting of a series of animal FAMILIES

Organism any member of the animal or plant kingdom; a body that has life

Ornithologist ZOOLOGIST specializing in the study of birds

Osteoderms bony plates beneath the scales of some REPTILES, particularly crocodilians

Oviparous producing eggs that hatch outside the body of the mother (in fish, REPTILES, birds, and MONOTREMES)

Parasite an animal or plant that lives on or within the body of another (the host) from which it obtains nourishment. The host is often harmed by the association

Passerine any bird of the ORDER Passeriformes; includes SONGBIRDS

Pedipalps small, paired leglike appendages immediately in front of the first pair of walking legs of spiders and other ARACHNIDS. Used by males for transferring sperm to the females

Pelagic living in the upper waters of the open sea or large lakes

Pheromone scent produced by animals to enable others to find and recognize them

Photosynthesis the production of food in green plants using sunlight as an energy source and water plus carbon dioxide as raw materials

Phylum zoological term for a major grouping of animal CLASSES. The whole animal kingdom is divided into about 30 PHYLA, of which the VERTEBRATES form part of just one

Placenta the structure that links an embryo to its mother during pregnancy, allowing exchange of chemicals between them

Plankton animals and plants drifting in open water; many are minute

Plastron the lower shell of CHELONIANS

Plumage the covering of feathers on a bird's body

Plume a long feather used for display, as in a bird of paradise

Polygamous where an individual has more than one mate in one BREEDING SEASON. Monogamous animals have only a single mate

Polygynous where a male mates with several females in one BREEDING SEASON

Polyp individual ORGANISM that lives as part of a COLONY—e.g., a coral—with a saclike body opening only by the mouth that is usually surrounded by a ring of tentacles

Population a distinct group of animals of the same SPECIES or all the animals of that SPECIES

Posterior the hind end or behind another structure

Predator an animal that kills live prey

Prehensile capable of grasping

Primary forest forest that has always been forest and has not been cut down and regrown at some time

Primates a group of MAMMALS that includes monkeys, apes, and ourselves

Prosoma the joined head and THORAX of a spider, scorpion, or horseshoe crab

Pupa an INSECT in the stage of METAMORPHOSIS between a caterpillar (LARVA) and an ADULT (imago)

Quadruped any animal that walks on four legs

Range the total geographical area over which a SPECIES is distributed

Raptor bird with hooked beak and strong feet with sharp claws (talons) for seizing, killing, and dealing with prey; also known as birds of prey. The term usually refers to daytime birds of prey (eagles, hawks, falcons, and relatives) but sometimes also includes NOCTURNAL owls

Regurgitate (of a bird) to vomit partly digested food either to feed NESTLINGS or to rid itself of bones, fur, or other indigestible parts, or (in some seabirds) to scare off PREDATORS

Reptile any member of the cold-blooded CLASS Reptilia, such as crocodiles, lizards, snakes, tortoises, turtles, and tuataras; characterized by an external covering of scales or horny plates. Most are egg-layers, but some give birth to fully developed young

Roost place that a bird or bat regularly uses for sleeping

Ruminant animals that eat vegetation and later bring it back from the stomach to chew again ("chewing the cud") to assist its digestion by microbes in the stomach

Savanna open grasslands with scattered trees and low rainfall, usually in warm areas

Scapulars the feathers of a bird above its shoulders

Scent chemicals produced by animals to leave smell messages for others to find and interpret

Scrub vegetation dominated by shrubs—woody plants usually with more than one stem

Scute horny plate covering live body tissue underneath

Secondary forest trees that have been planted or grown up on cleared ground

Sedge grasslike plant

Shorebird Plovers, sandpipers, and relatives (known as waders in Britain, Australia, and some other areas)

Slash-and-burn agriculture method of farming in which the unwanted vegetation is cleared by cutting down and burning

Social behavior interactions between individuals within the same SPECIES, e.g., courtship

Songbird member of major bird group of PASSERINES

Spawning the laying and fertilizing of eggs by fish and AMPHIBIANS and some mollusks

Speciation the origin of SPECIES; the diverging of two similar ORGANISMS

through reproduction down through the generations into different forms resulting in a new SPECIES

Species a group of animals that look similar and can breed with each other to produce fertile offspring

Steppe open grassland in parts of the world where the climate is too harsh for trees to grow

Subspecies a subpopulation of a single SPECIES whose members are similar to each other but differ from the typical form for that SPECIES; often called a race

Substrate a medium to which fixed animals are attached under water, such as rocks onto which barnacles and mussels are attached, or plants are anchored in, e.g., gravel, mud, or sand in which AQUATIC plants have their roots embedded

Substratum see SUBSTRATE

Swim bladder a gas or air-filled bladder in fish; by taking in or exhaling air, the fish can alter its buoyancy

Symbiosis a close relationship between members of two species from which both partners benefit

Taxonomy the branch of biology concerned with classifying ORGANISMS into groups according to similarities in their structure, origins, or behavior. The categories, in order of increasing broadness, are: SPECIES, GENUS, FAMILY, ORDER, CLASS, PHYLUM

Terrestrial living on land

Territory defended space

Test an external covering or "shell" of an INVERTEBRATE such as a sea-urchin; it is in fact an internal skeleton just below the skin

Thorax (**thoracic**, adj.) in an INSECT the middle region of the body between the head and the abdomen. It bears the wings and three pairs of walking legs

Torpor deep sleep accompanied by lowered body temperature and reduced METABOLIC RATE

Translocation transferring members of a SPECIES from one location to another

Tundra open grassy or shrub-covered lands of the far north

Underfur fine hairs forming a dense, woolly mass close to the skin and underneath the outer coat of stiff hairs in MAMMALS

Understory the layer of shrubs,

herbs, and small trees found beneath the forest CANOPY

Ungulate one of a large group of hoofed animals such as pigs, deer, cattle, and horses; mostly HERBIVORES

Uterus womb in which embryos of MAMMALS develop

Ultrasounds sounds that are too high-pitched for humans to hear

UV-B radiation component of ultraviolet radiation from the sun that is harmful to living ORGANISMS because it breaks up DNA

Vane the bladelike main part of a typical bird feather extending from either side of its shaft (midrib)

Ventral of or relating to the front part or belly of an animal (see DORSAL)

Vertebrate animal with a backbone (e.g., fish, MAMMAL, REPTILE), usually with skeleton made of bones, but sometimes softer cartilage

Vestigial a characteristic with little or no use, but derived from one that was well developed in an ancestral form; e.g., the "parson's nose" (the fatty end portion of the tail when a fowl is cooked) is the compressed bones from the long tail of the reptilian ancestor of birds

Viviparous (of most MAMMALS and a few other VERTEBRATES) giving birth to active young rather than laying eggs

Waterfowl members of the bird FAMILY Anatidae, the swans, geese, and ducks; sometimes used to include other groups of wild AQUATIC birds

Wattle fleshy protuberance, usually near the base of a bird's BILL

Wingbar line of contrasting feathers on a bird's wing

Wing case one of the protective structures formed from the first pair of nonfunctional wings, which are used to protect the second pair of functional wings in INSECTS such as beetles

Wintering ground the area where a migrant spends time outside the BREEDING SEASON

Yolk part of the egg that contains nourishment for a growing embryo

Zooid individual animal in a colony; usually applied to corals or bryozoa (sea-mats)

Zoologist person who studies animals

Zoology the study of animals

Further Reading

Mammals

Macdonald, David, *The Encyclopedia of Mammals*, Barnes & Noble, New York, U.S., 2001

Payne, Roger, *Among Whales*, Bantam Press, U.S., 1996

Reeves, R. R., and Leatherwood, S., *The Sierra Club Handbook of Whales and Dolphins of the World*, Sierra Club, U.S., 1983

Sherrow, Victoria, and Cohen, Sandee, *Endangered Mammals of North America*, Twenty-First Century Books, U.S., 1995

Whitaker, J. O., *Audubon Society Field Guide to North American Mammals*, Alfred A. Knopf, New York, U.S., 1996

Birds

Attenborough, David, *The Life of Birds*, BBC Books, London, U.K., 1998

BirdLife International, *Threatened Birds of the World*, Lynx Edicions, Barcelona, Spain and BirdLife International, Cambridge, U.K., 2000

del Hoyo, J., Elliott, A., and Sargatal, J., eds., *Handbook of Birds of the World* Vols 1 to 6, Lynx Edicions, Barcelona, Spain, 1992–2001

Sayre, April Pulley, *Endangered Birds of North America*, Scientific American Sourcebooks, Twenty-First Century Books, U.S., 1977

Scott, Shirley L., ed., *A Field Guide to the Birds of North America*, National Geographic, U.S., 1999

Stattersfield, A., Crosby, M., Long, A., and Wege, D., eds., *Endemic Bird Areas of the World: Priorities for Biodiversity Conservation*, BirdLife International, Cambridge, U.K., 1998

Thomas, Peggy, *Bird Alert: Science of Saving*, Twenty-First Century Books, U.S., 2000

Fish

Bannister, Keith, and Campbell, Andrew, *The Encyclopedia of Aquatic Life*, Facts On File, New York, U.S., 1997

Buttfield, Helen, *The Secret Lives of Fishes*, Abrams, U.S., 2000

Reptiles and Amphibians

Corbett, Keith, *Conservation of European Reptiles and Amphibians*, Christopher Helm, London, U.K., 1989

Corton, Misty, *Leopard and Other South African Tortoises*, Carapace Press, London, U.K., 2000

Hofrichter, Robert, *Amphibians: The World of Frogs, Toads, Salamanders, and Newts*, Firefly Books, Canada, 2000

Stafford, Peter, *Snakes*, Natural History Museum, London, U.K., 2000

Insects

Borror, Donald J., and White, Richard E., *A Field Guide to Insects: America, North of Mexico*, Houghton Mifflin, New York, U.S., 1970

Pyle, Robert Michael, *National Audubon Society Field Guide to North American Butterflies*, Alfred A. Knopf, New York, U.S., 1995

General

Adams, Douglas, and Carwardine, Mark, *Last Chance to See*, Random House, London, U.K., 1992

Allaby, Michael, *The Concise Oxford Dictionary of Ecology*, Oxford University Press, Oxford, U.K., 1998

Douglas, Dougal, and others, *Atlas of Life on Earth*, Barnes & Noble, New York, U.S., 2001

National Wildlife Federation, *Endangered Species: Wild and Rare*, McGraw-Hill, U.S., 1996

Websites

http://www.abcbirds.org/ American Bird Conservancy. Articles, information about campaigns and bird conservation in the Americas

http://elib.cs.berkeley.edu/aw/ AmphibiaWeb information about amphibians and their conservation

http://animaldiversity.ummz. umich.edu/ University of Michigan Museum of Zoology animal diversity web. Search for pictures and information about animals by class, family, and common name. Includes glossary

www.beachside.org sea turtle preservation society

http://www.birdlife.net BirdLife International, an alliance of conservation organizations working in more than 100 countries to save birds and their habitats

http://www.surfbirds.com Articles, mystery photographs, news, book reviews, birding polls, and more

http://www.birds.cornell.edu/ Cornell University. Courses, news, nest-box cam

http://www.cites.org/ CITES and IUCN listings. Search for animals by scientific name of order, family, genus, species, or common name. Location by country and explanation of reasons for listings

www.ufl.edu/natsci/herpetology/ crocs.htm crocodile site, including a chat room

www.darwinfoundation.org/ Charles Darwin Research Center

http://www.open.cc.uk/daptf DAPTF–Declining Amphibian Population Task Force. Providing information and data about amphibian declines. (International Director, Professor Tim Halliday, is co-author of this set)

http://www.ucmp.berkeley.edu/ echinodermata the echinoderm phylum—starfish, sea-urchins, etc.

http://endangered.fws.gov information about endangered animals and plants from the U.S. Fish and Wildlife Service, the organization in charge of 94 million acres of wildlife refuges

http://forests.org/ includes forest conservation answers to queries

www.traffic.org/turtles freshwater turtles

www.iucn.org details of species, IUCN listings and IUCN publications

http://www.pbs.org/journeytoama zonia the Amazonian rain forest and its unrivaled biodiversity

http://www.audubon.org National Audubon Society, named after the ornithologist and wildlife artist John James Audubon (1785–1851). Sections on education, local Audubon societies, and bird identification

www.nccnsw.org.au site for threatened Australian species

http://cmc-ocean.org facts, figures, and quizzes about marine life

http://wwwl.nature.nps.gov/wv/ The U.S. National Park Service wildlife and plants site. Factsheets on all kinds of animals found in the parks

www.ewt.org.za endangered South African wildlife

http://www.panda.org World Wide Fund for Nature (WWF). Newsroom, press releases, government reports, campaigns. Themed photogallery

http://www.greenchannel.com/ wwt/ Wildfowl and Wetlands Trust (U.K.). Founded by artist and naturalist Sir Peter Scott, the trust aims to preserve wetlands for rare waterbirds. Includes information on places to visit and threatened waterbird species

http://wdcs.org/ Whale and Dolphin Conservation Society site. News, projects, and campaigns. Sightings database

List of Animals by Group

Listed below are the common names of the animals featured in the A–Z part of this set grouped by their class, i.e., Mammals, Birds, Fish, Reptiles, Amphibians, and Insects and Invertebrates.

Bold numbers indicate the volume number and are followed by the first page number of the two-page illustrated main entry in the set.

Mammals

addax **2**:4
anoa, mountain **2**:20
anteater, giant **2**:24
antelope, Tibetan **2**:26
armadillo, giant **2**:30
ass
  African wild **2**:34
  Asiatic wild **2**:36
aye-aye **2**:42
babirusa **2**:44
baboon, gelada **2**:46
bandicoot, western barred **2**:48
banteng **2**:50
bat
  ghost **2**:56
  gray **2**:58
  greater horseshoe **2**:60
  greater mouse-eared **2**:62
  Kitti's hog-nosed **2**:64
  Morris's **2**:66
bear
  grizzly **2**:68
  polar **2**:70
  sloth **2**:72
  spectacled **2**:74
beaver, Eurasian **2**:76
bison
  American **2**:86
  European **2**:88
blackbuck **2**:94
camel, wild bactrian **3**:24
cat, Iriomote **3**:30
cheetah **3**:40
chimpanzee **3**:42
  pygmy **3**:44
chinchilla, short-tailed **3**:46
cow, Steller's sea **3**:70
cuscus, black-spotted **3**:86
deer
  Chinese water **4**:6
  Kuhl's **4**:8
  Père David's **4**:10
  Siberian musk **4**:12
desman, Russian **4**:14
dhole **4**:16
dog
  African wild **4**:22

bush **4**:24
dolphin
  Amazon river **4**:26
  Yangtze river **4**:28
dormouse
  common **4**:30
  garden **4**:32
  Japanese **4**:34
drill **4**:40
dugong **4**:46
duiker, Jentink's **4**:48
dunnart, Kangaroo Island **4**:50
echidna, long-beaked **4**:60
elephant
  African **4**:64
  Asian **4**:66
elephant-shrew, golden-rumped **4**:68
ferret, black-footed **4**:72
flying fox
  Rodrigues (Rodriguez) **4**:84
  Ryukyu **4**:86
fossa **4**:90
fox, swift **4**:92
gaur **5**:18
gazelle, dama **5**:20
gibbon, black **5**:26
giraffe, reticulated **5**:30
glider, mahogany **5**:32
gorilla
  mountain **5**:38
  western lowland **5**:40
gymnure, Hainan **5**:48
hare, hispid **5**:50
hippopotamus, pygmy **5**:52
horse, Przewalski's wild **5**:58
hutia, Jamaican **5**:64
hyena
  brown **5**:66
  spotted **5**:68
ibex, Nubian **5**:70
indri **5**:84
jaguar **5**:86
koala **6**:10
kouprey **6**:14
kudu, greater **6**:16
lemur
  hairy-eared dwarf **6**:22
  Philippine flying **6**:24
  ruffed **6**:26
leopard **6**:28
  clouded **6**:30
  snow **6**:32
lion, Asiatic **6**:34
loris, slender **6**:46
lynx, Iberian **6**:52
macaque
  barbary **6**:54
  Japanese **6**:56
manatee, Florida **6**:68
markhor **6**:72
marten, pine **6**:74
mink, European **6**:78

mole, marsupial **6**:80
mole-rat
  Balkans **6**:82
  giant **6**:84
monkey
  douc **6**:86
  Goeldi's **6**:88
  proboscis **6**:90
mouse, St. Kilda **6**:92
mulgara **6**:94
numbat **7**:14
nyala, mountain **7**:18
ocelot, Texas **7**:20
okapi **7**:22
orang-utan **7**:26
oryx
  Arabian **7**:28
  scimitar-horned **7**:30
otter
  European **7**:32
  giant **7**:34
  sea **7**:36
ox, Vu Quang **7**:44
panda
  giant **7**:48
  lesser **7**:50
pangolin, long-tailed **7**:52
panther, Florida **7**:54
pig, Visayan warty **7**:68
pika, steppe **7**:74
platypus **7**:82
porpoise, harbor **7**:86
possum, Leadbeater's **7**:88
potoroo, long-footed **7**:90
prairie dog, black-tailed **7**:92
pygmy-possum, mountain **8**:4
quagga **8**:8
rabbit
  Amami **8**:12
  volcano **8**:14
rat, black **8**:24
rhinoceros
  black **8**:26
  great Indian **8**:28
  Javan **8**:30
  Sumatran **8**:32
  white **8**:34
rock-wallaby, Prosperine **8**:36
saiga **8**:42
sea lion, Steller's **8**:62
seal
  Baikal **8**:70
  gray **8**:72
  Hawaiian monk **8**:74
  Mediterranean monk **8**:76
  northern fur **8**:78
sheep, barbary **8**:88
shrew, giant otter **8**:90
sifaka, golden-crowned **8**:92
sloth, maned **9**:6
solenodon, Cuban **9**:16
souslik, European **9**:18
squirrel, Eurasian red **9**:28

tahr, Nilgiri **9**:46
takin **9**:50
tamarin, golden lion **9**:52
tapir
  Central American **9**:56
  Malayan **9**:58
tenrec, aquatic **9**:64
thylacine **9**:66
tiger **9**:68
tree-kangaroo, Goodfellow's **10**:4
vicuña **10**:28
whale
  blue **10**:40
  fin **10**:42
  gray **10**:44
  humpback **10**:46
  killer **10**:48
  minke **10**:50
  northern right **10**:52
  sei **10**:54
  sperm **10**:56
  white **10**:58
wildcat **10**:62
wolf
  Ethiopian **10**:64
  Falkland Island **10**:66
  gray **10**:68
  maned **10**:70
  red **10**:72
wolverine **10**:74
wombat, northern hairy-nosed **10**:76
yak, wild **10**:90
zebra
  Grevy's **10**:92
  mountain **10**:94

Birds

akiapolaau **2**:6
albatross, wandering **2**:8
amazon, St. Vincent **2**:14
asity, yellow-bellied **2**:32
auk, great **2**:38
barbet, toucan **2**:54
bellbird, three-wattled **2**:82
bird of paradise, blue **2**:84
bittern, Eurasian **2**:90
blackbird, saffron-cowled **2**:92
bowerbird, Archbold's **3**:8
bustard, great **3**:10
cassowary, southern **3**:28
cockatoo, salmon-crested **3**:52
condor, California **3**:60
coot, horned **3**:62
cormorant, Galápagos **3**:64
corncrake **3**:66
courser, Jerdon's **3**:68
crane, whooping **3**:76
crow, Hawaiian **3**:82
curlew, Eskimo **3**:84
dipper, rufous-throated **4**:18

Set Index

A **bold** number indicates the volume number and is followed by the relevant page number or numbers (e.g., **1:**52, 74).

Animals that are main entries in the A–Z part of the set are listed under their common names, alternative common names, and scientific names. Animals that appear in the data panels as Related endangered species are also listed under their common and scientific names.

Common names in **bold** (e.g., **addax**) indicate that the animal is a main entry in the set. Underlined page numbers (e.g., **2:**12) indicate the first page of the two-page main entry on that animal.

Italic volume and page references (e.g., *1:57*) indicate illustrations of animals in other parts of the set.

References to animals that are listed by the IUCN as Extinct (EX), Extinct in the Wild (EW), or Critically Endangered (CR) are found under those headings.

spp. means species.

A

Aceros spp. **5:**56
  A. leucocephalus **5:**5
Acestrura bombus **4:**78
Acinonyx jubatus **3:**40
Acipenser
  A. nudiventris **9:**36
  A. sturio **9:**36
Acrantophis madagascariensis **3:**6
Acrocephalus spp. **10:**36
  A. paludicola **10:**36
adaptation, reproductive strategies **1:**25
addax 2:4
Addax nasomaculatus **2:**4
Adelocosa anops **9:**24
Adranichthyis kruyti **10:**88
Aegialia concinna **2:**80
Aegypius monachus **10:**34
Aepypodius bruijnii **6:**64
Afropavo congensis **7:**60
Agapornis
  A. fischeri **6:**48
  A. nigrigenis **6:**48
Agelaius xanthomus **2:**92
Aglaeactis aliciae **4:**78
agricultural land use **1:**38, 61
agricultural practices **1:**52, 74; **2:**60, 63, 73, 92; **3:**10, 13, 67, 85; **4:**19, 24, 75; **5:**50, 94; **6:**6, 36, 38, 48, 82, 95; **7:**12, 19; **8:**95; **9:**4, 18; **10:**14, 34
Ailuroedus dentirostris **3:**8
Ailuropoda melanoleuca **7:**48
Ailurus fulgens **7:**50
akiapolaau 2:6
ala Balik **8:**52
Alabama **3:**34
alala **3:**82
Alauda razae **6:**18

albatross
  various **2:**9
  wandering 2:8
Algeria **7:**16
alien species **1:**71; **2:**7, 56, 77; **3:**27, 65, 83; **4:**15, 20, 50, 76, 78, 79, 88; **5:**6, 11, 17, 22, 36, 43, 46, 50, 61, 64, 74, 76, 88, 92; **6:**8, 19, 62, 65, 78, 80, 94; **7:**5, 9, 10, 14, 59, 66, 70, 82, 90; **8:**12, 19, 20, 40, 16; **9:**9, 16, 28, 32, 38, 48, 72, 81, 88; **10:**60, 87, 88
Alligator
  A. mississippiensis **2:**10
  A. sinensis **2:**12
alligator
  American 2:10
  Chinese 2:12
Allocebus trichotis **6:**22
Allotoca maculata **5:**36
Alsophis spp. **8:**16
  A. antiguae **8:**16
Alytes muletensis **9:**72
Amandava formosa **4:**74
amarillo **5:**36
amazon
  St. Vincent 2:14
  various **2:**14
Amazona spp. **2:**14
  A. guildingii **2:**14
Amblyopsis
  A. rosae **3:**34
  A. spelaea **3:**34
Amblyornis flavifrons **3:**8
Amblyrhynchus cristatus **5:**78
Ambystoma
  A. macrodactylum croceum **8:**51
  A. mexicanum **2:**40
Amdystoma spp. **8:**44
  A. californiense **8:**44
Ameca splendens **5:**36

Ammotragus lervia **8:**88
amphibians **1:**76
  diversity **1:**76
  risks **1:**78
  strategies **1:**76
  see also List of Animals by Group, page 100
Anas spp. **9:**62
  A. formosa **9:**62
  A. laysanensis **7:**10
  A. wyvilliana **7:**10
anchovy, freshwater 2:16
Andes **2:**74; **3:**46; **4:**80; **10:**28
Andrias
  A. davidianus **8:**46
  A. japonicus **8:**46
anemone see sea anemone
angelfish
  masked 2:18
  resplendent pygmy **2:**19
Angola **10:**94
angonoka **9:**90
animal products **1:**46; **3:**28, 75; **10:**42, 58
anoa
  lowland **2:**20; **6:**14
  mountain 2:20
Anoa mindorensis **2:**20
Anodorhynchus spp. **6:**60
  A. hyacinthus **6:**58
Anser erythropus **7:**10
ant, European red wood 2:22
anteater
  banded **7:**14
  fairy **2:**25
  giant 2:24
  marsupial **7:**14
  scaly **7:**52
antelope 2:4, 26; **4:**48; **5:**20; **6:**16; **7:** 18, 28, 30; **8:**42
Anthornis melanocephala **5:**54
Anthracoceros
  A. marchei **5:**56
  A. montani **5:**56
Antigua **8:**16
Antilope cervicapra **2:**94
Antilophia bokermanni **6:**66
aoudad **8:**88
ape, barbary **6:**54
Aplonis spp. **9:**30
Apodemus sylvaticus hirtensis **6:**92
Apteryx spp. **6:**9
  A. mantelli **6:**8
aquaculture **8:**55
aquarium trade **1:**49; **4:**36; **8:**23, 69, 84
Aquila spp. **4:**56
  A. adalberti **4:**56
Aramidopsis plateni **3:**66
arapaima **7:**76
Arapaima gigas **7:**76
archerfish
  few-scaled **2:**28
  large-scaled **2:**28

  western **2:**28
Archiboldia papuensis **3:**8
archipelagos **1:**32
  see also islands
Arctic **2:**70
Arctic Ocean **10:**58
Arctocephalus spp. **8:**62, 78
Ardeotis nigriceps **3:**10
Argentina **3:**46; 62; **4:**18
Arizona **3:**60
armadillo
  giant 2:30
  various **2:**30
arowana, Asian **4:**36
artificial fertilization **1:**88
Asia **3:**10, 66; **6:**20
asity
  Schlegel's **2:**32
  yellow-bellied 2:32
Aspidites ramsayi **8:**6
ass
  African wild 2:34; **8:**8
  Asiatic wild 2:36; **8:**8
  half- **2:**36
  Syrian wild *1:37*
Astacus astacus **3:**78
Asterina phylactica **3:**88
Astyanax mexicanus **3:**38
Atelopus varius **5:**8
Atlantic Ocean **3:**54, 88; **8:**72, 76, 80; **9:**36; **10:**8, 40, 43
Atlantisia rogersi **3:**66
Atlapetes flaviceps **4:**76
Atrichornis
  A. clamosus **8:**56
  A. rufescens **8:**56
auk, great 2:38
aurochs *1:37*
Australia **2:**16, 28, 48, 56; **3:**16, 28; **4:**38, 46, 50, 58, 74, 94; **5:**12, 32, 54; **6:**10, 51, 64, 80, 94; **7:**14, 58, 82, 88, 90; **8:**4, 6, 36, 56; **9:**4, 66, 78; **10:**20, 22, 77
Austroglanis barnardi **3:**32
avadavat, green **4:**74
avahi **5:**84; **8:**93
Avahi occidentalis **5:**84; **8:**93
Axis kuhlii **4:**8
axolotl 2:40; **8:**44
aye-aye 2:42

B

babirusa 2:44
baboon, gelada 2:46
Babyrousa babyrussa **2:**44
baiji **4:**28
Balaenoptera
  B. acutorostrata **10:**50
  B. borealis **10:**54
  B. musculus **10:**40
  B. physalus **10:**42
Balantiocheilos melanopterus **8:**84
Balantiopteryx infusca **2:**64
Balearic Islands **6:**40; **9:**72

Bali **9:**30, 68
Baltic **8:**72; **9:**36
bandicoot
  eastern barred **2:**48
  golden **2:**48
  greater rabbit-eared *1:36*
  little barred **2:**48
  Shark Bay striped **2:**48
  western barred 2:48
Bangladesh **2:**72
banteng 2:50
barb
  bandula 2:52
  seven-striped **5:**82
  various **2:**52
barbet
  toucan 2:54
  various **2:**54
Barbus (Puntius) spp. **2:**52
  B. (P.) bandula **2:**52
bat
  Australian false vampire **2:**56
  ghost 2:56
  gray 2:58
  greater horseshoe 2:60
  greater mouse-eared 2:62
  Guatemalan **2:**62
  Indiana **2:**62
  Kitti's hog-nosed 2:64
  Morris's 2:66
  mouse-tailed **2:**64
  myotis, various **2:**66
  sheath-tailed **2:**64
  see also flying fox
Bawean Island **4:**8
bear
  Asian black **2:**68
  Asiatic black **2:**74
  brown **2:**68
  grizzly 2:68
  Mexican grizzly *1:37*; **2:**68
  polar 2:70
  sloth 2:72
  spectacled **2:**74
beaver, Eurasian 2:76
beetle
  blue ground 2:78
  Ciervo scarab **2:**80
  delta green ground **2:**78
  Giuliani's dune scarab **2:**80
  hermit 2:80
  longhorn **6:**44
  scarab **2:**80
behavior studies **1:**85
bellbird
  bare-throated **2:**82
  Chatham Island **5:**54
  three-wattled 2:82
Belontia signata **7:**56
beloribitsa **8:**52
beluga **10:**58
Bering Sea **8:**62
Bermuda **7:**66
bettong, northern **7:**90
Bettongia tropica **7:**90
Bhutan **8:**28; **9:**50
big-game hunting **1:**47; **9:**68

107

Acknowledgments

The authors and publishers would like to thank the following people and organizations: Aquamarines International Pvt. Ltd., Sri Lanka, especially Ananda Pathirana; Aquarist & Pond keeper Magazine, U.K.; BirdLife International (the global partnership of conservation organizations working together in over 100 countries to save birds and their habitats). Special thanks to David Capper; also to Guy Dutson and Alison Stattersfield; Sylvia Clarke (Threatened Wildlife, South Australia); Mark Cocker (writer and birder); David Curran (aquarist specializing in spiny eels, U.K.); Marydele Donnelly (IUCN sea turtle specialist); Svein Fossa (aquatic consultant, Norway); Richard Gibson (Jersey Wildlife Preservation Trust, Channel Islands); Paul Hoskisson (Liverpool John Moores University); Derek Lambert; Pat Lambert (aquarists specializing in freshwater livebearers); Lumbini Aquaria Wayamba Ltd., Sri Lanka, especially Jayantha Ramasinghe and Vibhu Perera; Isolda McGeorge (Chester Zoological Gardens); Dr. James Peron Ross (IUCN crocodile specialist); Zoological Society of London, especially Michael Palmer, Ann Sylph, and the other library staff.

Picture Credits

Abbreviations

AL   Ardea London
BBC   BBC Natural History Unit
BCC   Bruce Coleman Collection
FLPA   Frank Lane Photographic Agency
NHPA   Natural History Photographic Agency
OSF   Oxford Scientific Films
PEP   Planet Earth Pictures
b = bottom; c = center; t = top; l = left; r = right

Jacket

Ibiza wall lizard, illustration by Denys Ovenden from *Collins Field Guide: Reptiles and Amphibians of Britain and Europe*; Grevy's zebra, Stan Osolinski/Oxford Scientific Films; Florida panther, Lynn M. Stone/BBC Natural History Unit; silver shark, Max Gibbs/Photomax; blue whale, Tui de Roy/Oxford Scientific Films

5 A.N.T./NHPA; **6–7** Michael Fogden/OSF; **8** G.I. Bernard/NHPA; **9** Ian Beames/AL; **11** Michael Fogden/OSF; **14–15** Survival Anglia/John Harris/OSF; **17** John Cancalosi/BBC; **19** Kenneth W. Fink/AL; **21** Aqualog; **23** Max Gibbs/Photomax; **25** Derek Middleton/FLPA; **26–27** John Downer/OSF; **28–29** Stan Osolinski/OSF; **32–33** Konrad Wothe/OSF; **34–35** Richard Packwood/OSF; **39** Kevin Schafer/NHPA; **41** David Armitage; **42–43** Martyn Colbeck/OSF; **43** Animals Animals/Wilfred Schurig/OSF; **45** David M. Dennis/OSF; **47** Orion Press/BCC; **48–49** Jack Dermid/OSF; **51** David M. Dennis/OSF; **52–53** Okapia/Andreas Hartl/OSF; **54–55** Survival Anglia/Terry Andrewartha/OSF; **57** Ray Smith/BirdLife International; **59** Dennis R. Seaward; **60–61** R.L. Manuel/OSF; **63** Tom Ulrich/OSF; **67** Fredrik Ehrenstrom/OSF; **69** Bob Bowen/Andromeda Oxford Limited; **70–71** Martyn Colbeck/OSF; **72–73** Kenneth Day/OSF; **74–75** David B. Fleetham/OSF; **77** F. Di Domenico/Panda/FLPA; **78–79** Stephen Krasemann/NHPA; **80–81** Charles & Sandra Hood/BCC; **82–83** Animals Animals/Carl Roessler/OSF; **84–95** Max Gibbs/Photomax; **86–87** Tony Bomford/OSF; **89** Animals Animals/Barbara Wright/OSF; **93** David Haring/OSF; **95** BirdLife International.

Artists

Graham Allen, Norman Arlott, Priscilla Barrett, Trevor Boyer, Ad Cameron, David Dennis, Karen Hiscock, Chloe Talbot Kelly, Mick Loates, Michael Long, Malcolm McGregor, Denys Ovenden, Oxford Illustrators, John Sibbick, Joseph Tomelleri, Dick Twinney, Ian Willis